The New Americans
Recent Immigration and American Society

Edited by
Steven J. Gold and Rubén G. Rumbaut

A Series from LFB Scholarly

Educating Immigrants
Experiences of Second-Generation Iranians

Mitra K. Shavarini

LFB Scholarly Publishing LLC
New York 2004

Library of Congress Cataloging-in-Publication Data

Shavarini, Mitra K., 1962-
  Educating immigrants : experiences of second-generation Iranians /
Mitra K. Shavarini.
     p. cm. -- (The new Americans : recent immigration and American
society)
  Includes bibliographical references and index.
  ISBN 1-59332-054-X (alk. paper)
  1. Iranian Americans. 2. Children of immigrants--United States. 3.
Iranian Americans--Education. I. Title. II. Series: New Americans
(LFB Scholarly Publishing LLC)
  E184.I5S53 2004
  371.829'9155073--dc22

2004012668

ISBN 1-59332-054-X

Printed on acid-free 250-year-life paper.

Manufactured in the United States of America.

TABLE OF CONTENTS

v

Acknowledgements

This study would not have been possible without the intellectual support of Patricia Albjerg Graham, Judith D. Singer, and Marcelo Suárez-Orozco. I am grateful for their mentorship.

A New American

With the passage of the 1965 U. S. Immigration Act, the United States has attracted the largest and most diverse group of immigrants in its history. In the late 1970s and early 1980s, with the outbreak of the Iranian Revolution, the United States became host to yet another varied group of immigrants – Iranians. As with its multitude of predecessors, this group of immigrants would bring with them their own unique heritage and would etch out their own particular history in their new host country.

Their relatively short migration history reveals that this immigrant group has placed substantial emphasis on educational attainment -- their own, as well as, their children's. Recent U.S. Census data reveals that one in four Iranian-Americans holds a master's or a doctoral degree. This immigrant group is a prominent figure on faculty positions in some top-ranked academic institutions: Harvard, Yale, MIT, George Washington University, among hundreds of others. Educational aspirations and attainment persists to be a high goal. What seems to be interesting is how these educational ideals are being transferred to the new generation of Iranians reared in the United States. What factors prompt the children of Iranian immigrants to strive educationally?

1

In this book, I capture the voices of second-generation Iranian immigrants. It is a qualitative study of thirty undergraduate Iranian students in New England and New York, and aims to understand the factors that have contributed to their educational outlooks. It is a sample that captures the "internal diversity" of experiences among Iranians, particularly as it relates to their religious and ethnic backgrounds. Most studies of immigrants tend to obscure the variability of a group to its national or racial category, missing the nuances that exist within an immigrant group. There are at least eight religious-ethnic groups among Iranians: Muslim, Jews, Armenians, Assyrian Christians, Bahá'ís, Kurds, Turks, and Zoroastrians. Here, I explain about the experiences of four of these groups (Muslims, Jews, Bahá'ís, and Armenians). I find that the common denominator among this internally diverse immigrant group is their sustained pursuit of education.

Second-generation Iranians in this study were either born around the time of the 1979 Iranian revolution, or shortly thereafter, at the time of the American hostage crisis. They "came of age" in the United States where their heritage conjured images of the hostage crisis -- of flag burning zealots who had humiliated America in the global stadium. The newly installed Islamic Republic, intent on purging itself of Western influences, accused the United States as an "evil" empire. Mutual political hostility ensued with detrimental consequences. Iranians endured slurs, lost or found it hard to find jobs, and became the victims of hate crimes. In an inhospitable climate, first-generation Iranians weathered years in the US intent on eventually returning to their homeland, a goal that dimmed as their children beckoned them to accept United States as their permanent residence.

Twenty years later, as the first cohort of second-generation Iranians enter colleges and universities in the United States, one can begin to understand the shadow of insecurity and uncertainty that permeated their parents' settlement in this country. This new generation has not internalized their parents' apprehension of being "Iranians" in America. Rather, they have strategically used the combination of both cultures -- Iranian and American -- to advance themselves academically. Unlike their parents, most of these students drew strength from their Iranian background. They publicly declared their heritage as Iranian -- assertions that only a prior decade would have been unwelcome in American society.

The late 1990s were a period of optimism for Iranian-Americans. There were signs of improved US-Iran relations and gestures on the part of both countries seemingly shifted the American public's generally negative image of Iranians. For instance, in 1997, Iran elected a new moderate president, Mohammad Khatami, a sign that Iran was moving towards moderation and perhaps diplomacy. The Iranian soccer team played the United States before 65,000 fans in 1998 in Lyon, France, in the World Cup where for the first time in twenty years Iranians publicly waved the Iranian flag. The relations between the two culminated in yet another US-Iran soccer match in January of 2000. It was Iran's debut in the U.S. and the first meeting between the countries since the 1998 World Cup. Improved political relations continued in 1998: Iranians warmly greeted American wrestlers who traveled to Iran, surprising the American public. And, the Clinton administration lifted trade embargoes on Persian rugs and foods. Each of these events became a milestone in thawing the US-Iran relationship and positively altered U.S. perceptions about Iranians in the U.S.

In the late 1990s, several biographical accounts of Iranians were published and positively caught American public's attention (Asayesh' Saffron Skies: A Life Between Iran and America; Rachlin's The Heart's Desire; Bahrampour's To See and See Again: A Life in Iran and America; Karim and Khorrami's (eds.) A World Between). Moreover, Iranian-made movies were featured in, and praised by, mainstream cinemas (White Balloon, Children of Heaven, Color of Paradise, and A Time for Drunken

Horses). It seemed that Iranians were redeeming themselves and were beginning to alter their terrorist-like imagery.

In this study, I found that the late 1990s were also a time of optimism for second-generation Iranians. I found that this generation strategically drew upon two cultures -- Iranian and American -- to strengthen their pursuit of education. These "hyphenated Americans" balanced two cultures and despite negative stereotypes of Iranians, they wore their Iranian heritage with pride. And, by striving educationally, they attempted to combat their entrenched terrorist-like image.

The findings of this study encapsulate the Iranian-American educational experience in the late 1990s. As a researcher, however, I wonder how a relatively recent historical event may have altered the findings of this study. The data for this study were gathered before the September 11, 2001 attacks. As part of my doctoral studies, I had conducted the interviews, analyzed the data, written the findings, and graduated just three months short of that paralyzing day. Two years later, as I prepare to turn this dissertation into a book, I find one gaping hole in what I am about to present.

September 11th and its aftermath of hostility and scorn have breathed – once again -- grave concern into the lives of Middle Easterners, generally, and Iranians, specifically. Not only have Iranians felt the tremendous loss this country has bore with that heinous act, but have once again suffered the backlash of politics between the United States and Iran. Shortly after 9/11, President Bush declared Iran as a threat to world security calling it a nation on the "axis of evil." This time the US branded Iran as "evil," a political accusation that once again had social implications for Iranians in the United States.

Thus, I am left to question -- incorrigibly -- how would these second-generation Iranians discuss their experiences if the study were to be conducted after 9/11? In trying to understand how my "outcome" would have been shadowed or tainted by 9/11, I have been informally surveying

Iranian-Americans. I use "informally surveying" to refer to my collection of anecdotes concerning the thoughts, opinions and attitudes of Iranians since the September attacks. I have found that first-generation Iranians, particularly those who resided here during the hostage crisis, continue to feel uneasy in the United States. After 24 years, they continue to be tenuously distant from their host society. They explain that they continue to be regarded in this country by the politics of Iran rather than their accomplishments in this country. A post-9/11 comment by a successful business owner in the Boston area captures the sentiment of many first-generation Iranians. He states, "even though I have lived here for 25 years, I feel out of place ... my generation will never feel accepted."

In these recent anecdotes I have found that second-generation of Iranians who are in their early to mid-teens share some of their parents' cautious reservations. Perhaps as a result of 9/11 backlash, these younger Iranians are hiding their family background. At a Boston community event in fall of 2003, a fourteen-year-old Iranian girl says, "Americans look at you differently if they know you are a Middle Easterner." When they near the school grounds, she typically reminds her mother "no more Farsi." Hiding her mother tongue and her family heritage is her way of protecting herself in the American high school environment where her difference could socially oust her. She is cautious of revealing her Iranian nationality; a precaution that echoes first-generation Iranians' experiences during the hostage crisis.

Through my informal inquiry, I have also found that college-aged Iranians continue to assert their Iranian identity. As I discuss in this book, this generation is not ashamed to "hold up" their national background in the eyes of American society. They appear proud and committed to the accomplishments of their heritage. In a post-9/11 conversation with a sophomore college student studying in the Boston area I found that this generation is more determined than ever to challenge the negative images that haunt them in this society. Profoundly he states, "we have to prove it ... we have to carry the torch and show Americans that we are not terrorists." Perhaps by the time they reach college, second-generation Iranians understand the paradox of their Iranian-American hyphenation. As Iranians, they are proud of their heritage; as Americans, they feel entitled to this nation; and as immigrants, they believe they have to work hard to prove themselves.

The above anecdotes illuminate how some of my findings may have been different had this study been conducted after 9/11. Indeed, the bold and daring emerging Iranian-American generation may have appeared more subdued and more concerned about their "place" in American society. However, they may have also been more determined than ever to correct the society that defines them. I believe that if the study were to be conducted today, I would find a similar educational conviction among Iranians as I did when I collected the data. Iranian immigrants' second-generation, reared and coming of age in the United States, continue to hold a strong belief in education that was also evident in the lives of their parents before migration. This book serves to illuminate what factors have led to this continued belief in the power of education.

CHAPTER ONE

Origins

The Iranian immigrant experience begins with a discussion of *where* this group came from and *why* they came -- a discussion that focuses on a brief snapshot of Iran's history, the period between 1963 and 1999. As is the case with any country, particularly one with a history spanning 2,500 years, there are many angles – political, economic, social, cultural – and/or institutions – religion, government, education – from which one can discuss/describe its history. Here, I focus on one institution – education – which I believe draws together the factors that are necessary to understand the context of the lives of Iranians living in the United States today. I use the lens of education because both the Pahlavi regime (1963-1979) and the subsequent Islamic Republic (1979-present) governments have used education as a vital institution through which to control Iran economically, politically, socially, and culturally. And it is precisely the combined effects of these controls that still resonate in the lives of today's Iranian immigrants in the United States.

An Ancient Land

Iran is a country of 627,000 square miles, the size of California, Texas, New Mexico, and Arizona combined. It borders Russia to the north, Iraq in the west, Turkey in the northwest, Afghanistan in the northeast, and Pakistan in the east. Iran's southern border runs along the coast of the Persian Gulf. Though it has never been the formal colony of any country, Iran has been vulnerable to pressures from both Russia and Britain.

Ancient Iran, vast and powerful, had an estimated 40 million people during the Safavid dynasty.[1] Throughout the centuries, wars and famines reduced this number to about 7.5 million at the beginning of twentieth century. Since then, Iran's population has continued to increase. In 1963, Iran's population was 23 million, and on the eve of the Iranian Revolution it was 34 million.[2] Twenty years after the Revolution, journal data show that the population is 62 million.[3] One of the world's youngest populations, 65 percent of Iranians are under the age of twenty-five (Wright, 1999).

One unique feature of Iran is its religious, ethnic, and linguistic diversity.[4] Before the Islamic Revolution, the population included approximately 250,000 Armenians and some 25,000 Nestorian Christians; 50,000 Protestants and Roman Catholics; 80,000 Jews; an estimated 60,000 Bahá'ís; and about 30,000 Parsis, Iranians who still hold to the religion of Zoroaster.[5] Some of the major ethnic groups in Iran include the Gilani and Mazandaranis, the Kurds, the Turks, the Lurs, the Bakhtiaris, and the Baluchis. And although Iran is often represented in literature as linguistically homogeneous, only about half of the total population speak Farsi as their first tongue, an Indo-European language. Languages in Iran are generally divided by linguists into two: Western (Gilaki, Mazandari, Tajik, Tati, Talishi, and Kirmanji, Baluchi, Parachi, Ormuri, Luri, Sivandi, Gabri, and Qumzari dialects) and Eastern groups (Afghi, Ossetic, Yaghnobi, Munjani, and Pamiri) (Nyrop, 1978).

Historical Overview of Education in Iran

Iran's educational history is rooted in the Achaemenid Empire (546 BCE to 330 BCE) and the Sassanian Dynasty (226 A.D. to 641 A.D.). During Iran's early history, people considered education an integration of family, community, and the state, and they sought to foster citizens who were religious, moral, and patriotic. For instance, the Zoroastrian doctrine – "A good mind should have a healthy body to live in" – was the essence of early Iranian education.

After the Arab invasion in 642 A.D. and the imposition of the Muslim religion, Iranian education changed radically. Whereas in Europe education was based on the Bible, Iran's system of education became based on the Islamic holy book, *Qoran*. In exchange for small sums of money from private and religious foundations, local communities established elementary schools called *maktab*. It was in these *maktabs* that upper- and middle-class urban youth -- the children of landlords, government officials, shopkeepers, and business people -- were educated by mullahs, Moslem clergymen. The curriculum, based on rote learning, primarily taught children to memorize the *Qoran*, along with some basic reading, writing, and arithmetic skills. Occasionally girls were allowed to attend *maktab*, but only those taught by a woman. Iranian higher education during the early years under Islam took the form of theological seminaries, or *elmieh*, where men gathered to interpret the *Qoran*, its philosophy and its implications of law. There was no place for women in this system of education. This general condition continued largely unchanged for centuries.

In 1828 Iran was defeated by Russia, and her sovereignty was pulled between Russian and British interests. Nasir Al-Din Shah, wanting to maintain control of his unruly, disorganized, and financially bereft army, assigned his administratively astute advisor, Amir Kabir, to the task of reorganizing the Iranian army. Arasteh (1969) hypothesizes that "the government's need for a bureaucratic administration directly brought about a system of higher education geared to the production of trained government personnel, who lacked, however, research or professional aims" (p. 27).

Amir Kabir, side-stepping the Anglo-Russian rivalry, contracted with Austria to help build its first institution of higher learning – one not fashioned for theology. In 1851, *Dar al-Fonun*, or House of Learning College, opened its doors to its first class of 105 students. The students chosen to attend were the children of aristocrats, landlords, and top government officials. They were boys between the ages of fourteen and sixteen and were enrolled for six years or more of tuition-free studies in the following fields: army science (61), engineering and mining (12), medicine (20), chemistry and pharmacy (7), and mineralogy (5) (Arasteh, 1969). French was the language of instruction since the entire faculty was either European or was educated in Europe, and French was the most widely used language among them.

Iran's ministry of education was founded in 1855 and modeled after the French educational system. Although the model was French, there were American, Russian, German, and British schools all over the country. By appropriating these Anglo-European models, however, Iran failed to establish a model that properly fit its own social context. (This issue is addressed in greater detail below.)

Until the 1920s, formal education in Iran was mainly based on the Islam (Shi'ite) religion. Only a small number of children were educated, and those who were schooled by and large tended to be males. Unlike Western countries where the government controlled the education system, in traditional Muslim societies during this time the clergy controlled education. The efforts of the Pahlavi dynasty[6] in the 1930s to promote mass education was the government's means of stripping the clergy of their control over the education system.

Reza Shah (reign: 1925-1941), the first reigning Shah of the Pahlavi dynasty, initiated a turf battle over the control of education by propagating the state's European-style secular ideology via a new system of national education. His Ministry of Education set up a non-religious system of co-ed national primary and secondary schools that was a "radical departure from tradition" (Arjomand, 1988, p. 68). In 1935, Iran's first university, University of Tehran, opened its doors to both men and women. The government also regularly sent students abroad for higher education. The aim of the new education system was to secularize the traditionally religious system, as a means of Westernizing Iran, suppressing Islam, promoting modernization, and instilling political support (Arjomand, 1988; Keddie, 1981; Mojab, 1991; Rucker, 1991).

The clergy, whose monopoly over education began to shatter, scrambled to regain control. They proposed that the government should at least hand over the responsibility for the administration of education and the religious endowments to the religious clergy -- ulama -- and allow them a few hours of radio time (Bakhash, 1986). Reza Shah, cognizant of the clergy's desire to reach the populace through the educational system, denied them all access. He believed that to actualize his dream of modernizing Iran he needed to repress the spread of traditional religious practices, particularly in the realm of education. In the early part of the century, circa the 1920's, Iranian youth were primarily enrolled in only the traditional primary and secondary schools. By the early 1960's, however, traditional schools were virtually eliminated; replaced by Reza Shah's modernized (secular) version of schooling. Over the course of forty years, elementary and secondary education in Iran had shifted from religious schools to modern schools (Arasteh, 1969; Fattahipour Fard, 1963).

Reza Shah's education reform plan became the basis for his son's -- Mohammed Reza -- efforts to modernize Iran. In the period after World War II, as the Western world preached "investment in education" as a strategy for modernization for the Third World, Iran fueled its already rigorous emphasis on education.

1963-1973: Iran's White Revolution

The notion that education raises one's status is widely embraced in many developing nations (Coleman, 1965; Coombs, 1985). Striving for a developed, industrialized state, developing nations have hastily subscribed to Western education models in order to improve their economies, failing to weigh the broader cultural and political consequences. In Iran, whose ancient history already exalted education, the "magic" of education became even more powerful during the quest for modernization. Menashri (1992) writes,

> In my travels in different regions of the country (mainly in Lorestan, Kurdistan, Fars, Mazanderan, Gilan, and Isfahan), I was impressed by the fact that education was held in high regard even in the most remote regions. The most striking example I came across was the small village of Razun in Lorestan. The village had no running water, no electricity, no sanitation, not even a public *hamam* (bath house). Yet when I asked the villagers what they needed most, they had only one answer: "The only thing we really need is a school. Only that can assure our children a better life than ours (p. 170).

The urban middle class and the elite had a similar attitude toward the value of education in the Iranian society. This high regard for education has historically been a common thread throughout the Iranian social fabric. Rural folks saw it "as a way to secure themselves a better life," more so than for "a better income" (Kinnane, 1971); middle classes saw education as the only means toward upper social and economic mobility; while for upper classes education secured their status quo.

The Shah believed that the secret to Western economic and military strength lay in their system of education. By imitating the West, he aimed to free Iran from underdevelopment and declare it a major global player. The

Shah symbolized education as the "national ship" (*kashti-ye vatan*) that would steer the country toward the "shore of progress" (*pishraft*). He considered the "holy duty" (*vazife-ye moqaddas*) of education to be spreading patriotism, not Islam. The education he propounded was secular and nationalistic, and Western in form and content. This attempt at transformation was not without its complications. Imitating the Western educational system would mean Iran would have to suppress traditional religious powers.

The bloody events of early 1963 illustrate the tensions between the Shah's secular government and the religious factions. Ironically, even the clerics who opposed modern education realized its social powers of transformation. In March 1963, on the anniversary of the martyrdom of the sixth Imam, Ja'far as Sadeq, paratroopers and SAVAK[7] attacked a religious school in Qom as a way of quelling the noticeably increased activities of religious schools. Several students were killed and their preacher, Ayatollah Khomeini, was arrested. The event was quelled and Khomeini was released after a brief detention. Throughout 1963, Khomeini denounced both America's role in Iran and its support of Israel. On June 4th, on the anniversary of the martyrdom of Imam Hosain.[8] Khomeini was arrested before dawn.[9] News quickly spread to Tehran, Shiraz, Kashan, and Mashhad universities, where holy processions quickly turned into political demonstrations. Religious propaganda calling for a Holy War circulated amongst the students. The demonstrations lasted several days – and claimed several hundred lives -- before the Shah was able to suppress the upheaval. The repercussions of these bloody exchanges would continue for years to come.

Ascending Towards Modernization

These religious tensions came at a time when Iran could be characterized as a nation racing to become modernized and obsessed with gaining military strength. Between 1963 and the early 1970s, oil revenues had given the Iranian economy its first dramatic boom. For example, in the period of four years (1968 and 1972) oil revenues had increased from $853.5 to $2,460.2 million. The rapid growth in the economy expanded the size of the government. The Ministry of Economics had already tripled in size while the ministries of education and agriculture doubled – increasing the demand for skilled and educated personnel to implement the new reforms (Bill, 1972). By 1963, the percentage of civil service employees with a higher education had increased from eight percent in previous years to over 21 percent. Thus, the government had nearly tripled its demand for more highly educated servants.[10]

This rapid economic expansion based on US-sponsored modernization policies transformed education, economic, and legal institutions. The shift that affected all these institutions required that the educational system, originally based on a French model, be fundamentally reformed (Menshari, 1992). Iran's system of higher education was the first to be reformed when the Shah ordered the establishment of the Pahlavi University (1962) to counterbalance the French system of instruction prevalent in Iranian universities of the time. With all instruction in English, American professors were recruited to its campus in Shiraz and close ties with American universities began to develop. Damavand College, for example, was spearheaded by the American scholar, Mary Catherine Bateson.

The shift toward an American educational model took a more comprehensive form by the late 1960s. Based on the advice of American consultants, Iran adopted a three-tiered model: elementary school (five years), intermediate school (three years), and high school (four years) (Arasteh, 1969; Menshari, 1992; Wilber, 1981). Again, however, these changes did not take into consideration Iran's particular needs for its educational system. Rather, they were Western educational models imported in the country's efforts toward development. Education was at the center of the country's efforts to achieve its economic goals, a notion that had taken a stronghold in the psyche of the nation. One can see the growing importance of, and participation in, education by comparing the growth of elementary and secondary education with Iran's population growth. In a little over thirty years, the percentage of the population that was enrolled in primary and secondary schools had expanded tenfold, see table 1 below. Although the expansion of education was partly fueled by the literacy corps and the compulsory education law(s),[11] one could argue that it was the growing public knowledge of the importance of education for the future of Iran that contributed to the burgeoning enrollment rates (see Menashri, 1992).

Table 1: Students at Elementary Schools in Selected Years

Year	Estimated population (in thousands)	No. of elementary and secondary students	No. of students as % of population
1941/2	12,833	315,355	2.46
1951/2	16,237	834,434	5.14
1961/2	22,372	1,733,986	7.75
1970/71	30,020	4,729,760	15.75
1977/78	36,000	7,701,000	21.39

Source: Menashri, 1992, p. 191.

The Ministry of Education was under increasing pressure to meet the growing demands placed on the school system. Though schools and universities were quickly erected to house the incoming masses of students, only a small segment of the entire population benefited, those living in urban areas. In the early 1970s, more than 68 percent of the Iranian population lived in towns and villages with populations of less than five thousand, yet there were less than a half dozen secondary schools available to them (Zonis, 1971). Even though two-thirds of the population lived in rural areas, differences in attendance rates between urban and rural areas were striking -- in urban areas 70 percent of children attended primary school, as opposed to 15 percent of rural children (Arasteh, 1969; Menashri, 1992). Rural students in Iran were virtually restricted to an education ending at the primary level during this period. Educational access in rural areas was one factor, coupled with failed land reform policies,[12] that prompted many people to migrate to urban centers.

Table 2: University Entrance Examinations: Number of Examinees and Number and Percentage Accepted, 1963-1969 (Includes figures for ten Iranian universities, including Tehran, Mashad, Tabriz, and Isfahan Universities)

Year	Examinees	Accepted	Percent Accepted
1963	18,000	2,050	11%
1964	29,335	4,000	14%
1966	35,000	4,000	11%
1969	60,000	8,000	13%
1970	64,000	8,990	14%
1972	80,000	10,000	13%

Source: *Kayhan,* Tehran, Iran: *Muassasah-i Kayhan*; also see Menashri, 1992; Zonis, 1971.

Rural families flocked to urban areas in hopes of giving their children a high school education, yet secondary education in Iran during the Shah's modernizing period was impractical (Arasteh, 1969; Menshari, 1992). Its sole purpose was to prepare students for the university entrance examination, not for the realities of their changing society. Iranian universities could only accept 10 percent of those who applied for admission, and those who could not pass the examination faced a bleak future during a modernizing era. In Iran's highly stratified society, higher education credentials were glorified: access to postsecondary education was closely associated with social status, acceptance, and economic mobility.

The following example illustrates the nature of this limited access to higher education in Iran during this time. The number of students who took the national university exam and the number (and percentage) who were accepted is shown for selected years in this time period in Table 2. It should be noted that the number of examinees includes those who had previously taken the exam and had been denied access to universities in former years. For example, in 1964, the pool of applicants included 11,825 individuals who had graduated from secondary schools in June of that year, and 17,150 who had failed the exam in previous years. Of those, 4,000, or 14 percent, of the applicants passed the entrance examination. By 1970, 64,000 took the exam and about 9,000 (still 14 percent) of the applicants were accepted. The absolute number of students was rising sharply yet the systems ability to absorb students remained about the same.

With such an intense emphasis on attaining higher education credentials, the portion of those who were unable to gain access were placed in a precarious position. These youth, who were not able to gain entry to a university, represented an increasingly disenchanted segment of Iran's society during this time. Unable to find employment in a rapidly modernizing society, these frustrated youth sowed the seeds of political unrest in succeeding years. What Iran needed to do was to expand its system of higher education – to build new universities and technical-vocational schools. Yet government policy restricted entrance to Iranian universities to the political and social elite. Zonis (1971) claims, based on a personal interview with an Iranian official who formulated higher education policies in Iran during the 1960s, that the ministry was given "orders" to restrict access to higher education. Both the cost of higher education and entrance examination standards were to remain high in order to limit the number of university students. Zonis also indicates that restricting access to the system of higher education was the government's misguided effort to maintain the status quo, while others claim it was the Shah's effort to control university campuses (Bill, 1972).

In Iran, obtaining a higher education credential was decidedly prestigious; it was a symbol of social achievement or status. Since access to it was also extremely restricted, tertiary education was highly correlated with class. Zonis (1971), using census data, shows that 85 percent of the population could neither read nor write.

Table 3: Highest Educational Level Achieved

Education	Total Iranian Population (N = 6,542,181)
No formal education	83.2%
Elementary	12.2%
Secondary	4.1%
University or post-secondary	0.4%
Post-graduate	0.1%
Total	100.0%

Source: Zonis, 1971, p.168 (Note: these figures are for males only.)

Yet, the education of elites was astoundingly high -- over 91 percent of Iran's elite had a university education. Table 3 shows that less than one half of one percent of the Iranian population had university or postsecondary education.

Because Iran could not absorb the majority of its secondary school graduates into its system of higher education, many upper-class Iranians sought education abroad. France and the United States competed for these students. Western education was highly regarded in Iran, and those who returned were often bestowed the title of "doctor," regardless of their degree or the institution at which they had studied. The prestige attached to a university diploma was even greater for a foreign degree (Arasteh, 1969). In 1964, there were 19,500 Iranian students studying in twenty-three foreign countries. By

1968 there were 25,000; only about 10 percent of these students were subsidized by the government,[13] the majority being independently financed (Arasteh, 1969; Wilber, 1981).

As increasing numbers of Iranians left to seek their education abroad, greater numbers also refused to return to Iran. The brain drain that this situation created exacerbated Iran's dire need for trained and skilled individuals. By 1965, the government had begun producing movies and special magazines urging Iranians to return to Iran after completing their studies. Many who did return to Iran were critical of, if not antagonistic toward, the Shah's regime (Ghods, 1989; Menashri, 1992; Wilber, 1981; Zonis, 1971). While they gained materially and socially under the Shah's reign, they were known to be frustrated with the political system, employment, and social issues.

During Iran's rapid ascent toward modernization, the country's infrastructure could be described as undeveloped, chaotic, and non-cohesive -- as evidenced by its troubled education system. Higher education was geared toward fulfilling civil service positions; secondary education benefited those preparing to go to college; elementary education was basically provided for the urban population. In sum, it was a system that met neither the needs of society nor the economy. It was a system that propelled Iranians to look to the West if they were to have any hopes of obtaining an education. It is during this time that Western education, particularly its system of higher education, began to become increasingly coveted by Iranians.

1973-1979: The Boom Years

By 1973, Iran's socioeconomic climate came to a critical juncture. Major problems included a youth population explosion; rapid industrialization; rapid urbanization (Iran's traditionally rural population, which could no longer sustain itself agriculturally, migrated to cities); rapid modernization; and rapid expansion of primary and secondary education and the inability of higher education to sustain growth. These problems existed within the context of Iran's booming, yet unstructured, oil revenue expenditures, which exacerbated its widening social gap, rapid inflation, and the spread of corruption.

For instance, during the 1970s, the energy crisis in the West led to soaring oil prices, which dramatically increased Iran's revenues. Between 1973 and 1975, Iran's oil revenues quintupled. Burgeoning revenues prompted the Shah to dramatically increase imports of construction materials and consumer goods from the West. Yet, Iran's underdeveloped infrastructure could not handle the import binge. Ships had to wait more than five months to unload their cargoes, and once they were unloaded there was no place to warehouse the goods. Automobile and tractor factories were built, but the human resources necessary to operate the technology were not readily available; assembling goods in Iran cost more than importing the finished product from the West. U.S. style supermarkets were built, threatening the small, traditional shopkeepers. Iran's system of education had not been designed to accommodate a rapid economic boom by providing the human resources needed to sustain the growth. Rather, it was designed after Western education models that sought to prepare youth for postsecondary education -- a misguided attempt toward development. Oil-derived subsidies did not increase efficiency and/or productiveness; instead, they made Iran dependent on the West.

Iran's dramatic economic changes were accompanied by various social changes. In large cities, people raced to acquire new and better housing, modern appliances, cars, and status clothes. While Iranians purchased symbols of the West and therefore modernization, a deeper acquisition of Western culture/values did not follow. Graham (1978) astutely points out that Iran's embrace of modern Western culture was superficial, as evidenced by two indices -- the publishing industry and the state of the university:

Despite a sharp increase in the number of people able to read and write, the number of titles published is in decline. Between 1970 and 1976 the number of titles and reprints published annually dropped by almost 30 percent. In 1976, only 3,200 titles were published, of which 1,580 were new (accounted for 36 percent by literary books and 18 percent by religious subjects.) The levels of titles published is infinitely lower than in nations of similar size like Turkey or Egypt (Graham, 1978, p. 200).

What Graham observed is that, although the economy was booming, the people were not becoming more educated.

Yet, there was continued pressure to seek entrance to the university system since financial and social mobility depended on it. By 1976, university enrollment had reached 154,000 students (110,000 male, 40,000 female). Some fields, such as medicine, that combined financial and social respectability became highly coveted, as though there were a "special mystique" about studying medicine. Competition in this field was fierce. For instance, 45,000 students competed for 300 total college seats in the field of medicine in 1977 (Graham, 1978).

The political and economic pressures created by the system of higher education outweighed its related social problems. If Iran were to integrate the technology it was importing, it needed institutions of higher education to produce a cadre of technically skilled citizens. Yet, the size and the quality of Iran's system of education was sacrificed in order for the Shah to maintain the status quo and thus preserve the stability of the regime. Universities were kept under strict political control and, as student hostility grew during the 1970s, they were frequently closed to subdue demonstrations and strikes (Graham, 1978; Wilber, 1981).

In addition to the growing dissent among college students there was increasing dissatisfaction among college administrators who were expected to expand the university annually with limited human resources and budgets. For example, in 1976 the educational system needed 40,000 new teachers a year but only had the capability of supporting half that number (Menashri, 1992). The student-teacher ratio had risen to 100 to 1. The Shah was more adamant about expanding military and policing powers than about addressing problems with the education system. Around 1977, two-thirds of Iran's population of 35 million were under sixteen. As these children approached adolescence, they would be pulled between the government's modern society and their families' traditional lives. What these youth understood is that their future in a traditional rural life was no longer economically feasible and that their only hopes of survival rested on gaining an education, primarily a college education. With this powerful social message inculcated in them, rural youth began migrating to Iran's cities. Coming from small towns, these lower-middle-class youth were the first in their families to come to the city, to attend a university, or both (Keddie, 1981; Menashri, 1992). The social pressures placed on these youth were invariably overwhelming. Menashri (1992), citing newspaper reports, states that the suicide rates among 16 to 20-year-olds were exceptionally high, particularly among urban youth who came from traditional religious families.[14] These disenfranchised youth had been pushed to gain a postsecondary education: their secondary education was designed to prepare them for their college entrance examination. Yet, they were competing for access to a structure that was able to accommodate only 10 percent of the college-age population. Without a college education, they had no training to participate in Iran's rapid economic development.

Confronted by an overwhelmingly secular urban environment, these impressionable young people assuaged their feelings of cultural displacement in religious organizations that had sprouted all over college campuses (Keddie, 1981). Campus religious organizations had a natural appeal to the city's newcomers, since the Shah's secularized urban lifestyle failed to accommodate them. This was one of the first signs that Iran's rapture with Western ideals and rapid economic growth was at odds with a major portion of the Iranian public.

The Economic Boom Yields Social Problems

By 1977, overcrowded urban centers, a widening income gap, conspicuous Western-style consumption by the elite, and the lack of political freedom were widely felt all over the nation. As occurred in other countries (e.g., China or, more recently, Indonesia), Iranian students -- young and idealistic, both at home and abroad – forged the voice of opposition to the Shah's regime.

Both the university entrance examinations and the shortage of professors fueled the exodus of unprecedented numbers of students to universities abroad. By 1978, their numbers reached 60,000. Forty percent of this group were enrolled in schools in the United States, where they constituted the largest foreign student population (Fereshteh, 1987). Ironically, a significant portion of the students studying in other nations would coalesce in opposition to the Shah. By denying them an education in their own homeland, the Shah had, in effect, created an ideal venue to foster opposition.[15] Free from the watchful eye of SAVAK, the propaganda of student organizations abroad would be first to inform the West of the Shah's human-rights violations. The Shah banned these student organizations, but though many were scared off by the regime's threats, the majority continued to work toward its downfall (Keddie, 1981).

The revolutionary movement was nowhere more evident than on the campuses of Iranian universities. Each building played host to various political factions vying for political power on the eve of the Iranian Revolution. On the campus of Tehran University, for example, the Organization of the People's Mujahedin set up its headquarters in the Faculty of Sciences, the Organization of

People's Fad'ian Guerillas was in the Faculty of Engineering, and the university mosque became the headquarters for "Imam's committee" (Behdad, 1995). Universities were virtually closed for the entire year prior to the Revolution.

Omens of what the Revolution was about to bring forth in Iranian society were found in graffiti on walls in Iranian cities that called for the death of Zoroastrians, Jews, Assyrians, and Armenians. These religious minorities feared what an Islamic society would mean for their futures. From his exile in Paris, Khomeini denounced Bahá'ís, but said that all other religious minorities would be protected. Despite Khomeini's assurances, Jews were skeptical of their future in Iran under an Islamic government since Khomeini had used anti-Zionist and anti-Israeli rhetoric throughout the revolutionary period. Fischer (1980) estimates that five to ten thousand of the eighty thousand Iranian Jews living in Iran left during the turmoil, many hoping to return.

The revolutionary riots of November 5, 1978, took to the street Khomeini's words regarding religious minorities. During the riot in Tehran that took down Reza Shah's statue in the center of the city, Armenian liquor stores were destroyed, yet all of the Jewish carpet shops were left untouched. The Armenian bishop immediately calmed the alarmed Christian-Iranian community, saying that the destruction was anti-liquor not anti-Armenian. To support the movement, some Christian Armenians took to the streets and chanted, Our religion is Christianity, Our leader is Khomeini (Fischer, 1980).

Zoroastrians and Sunni minorities also showed concern about what the future government would have in store for them. During the revolutionary riots, Islamic militants marched into the Zoroastrian fire temples and removed portraits of their prophet, replacing it with Khomeini's picture. The case of the Kurds and Sunni minorities in the south of Iran illustrates the complexities of issues -- ethnicity, religion, and language – in this revolutionary period (see earlier discussion in this chapter regarding ethnicity, religion, and language in Iran). On January 16, 1979, ending forty years of Pahlavi rule, the Shah went into exile. Two weeks later, on February 2, 1979, Ayatollah Ruhollah Khomeini returned to Iran after fifteen years in exile and subsequently changed the course of Iranian history. Some have described the change between the governments as one of Iran's most stunning political changes (Ghods, 1989; Keddie, 1981; Zabih, 1982). And Menashri (1992) writes that "the educational system, as hitherto a major, if not the major, instrument for advancing westernization, now came to be regarded as a tool for advancing 'Islamization'" (p. 6).

1979- 1988: The Imam Replaces the Shah

When Khomeini came to power in 1979, religious leaders wrote a new constitution. It declared that everyone had the right to a free education through high school (Article 36). The constitution also recognized issues of equality due to ethnicity, religion, family background, or tribal origin (Article 14).[16] The Revolutionary movement was similar to movements fighting apartheid and colonial rule in Africa, military dictatorships in Latin America, and Communism in Eastern Europe. The Iranian people wanted basic human rights and to determine their individual and national destinies.

Yet, Khomeini's vision for his new government differed from that of the general populace. His domestic and foreign policy embodied sentiments of a unitary Islamic state, and to achieve his goal, his new government would began an "Islamization" process that was intended to shape new generations with an "Islamic personality." Just as other faiths -- Christianity, Judaism, Buddhism, Hinduism – have used their ideology to shape political movements, Khomeini used Islam to shape a new order. He suspended Family Protection Law, outlawed coeducation, and banned women magistrates. Islamic law and judges were reestablished; liquor, gambling, and music were all outlawed. And, the educational system was "Islamicized" at all levels. Again, Iran's system of education was used at the behest of the government to change Iran's social structure. Islamization would also ensure that all forms of ideology would adhere to an Islamic state. Several months after Khomeini came to power, ethnic and religious minorities began to assert their frustration that Khomeini only spoke of a Shi'ite state. Iranian ethnic minorities – Kurds, Turkomans, the Arabs of Khuzistan, and the Baluchis – had supported Khomeini's revolution. The Pahlavis had discouraged the use of ethnic languages in either schools or the publication of literature, and had appointed their own officials (governors, military personnel, etc.) rather than allowing local leaders to govern. Ethnic minorities now wanted to run their schools using their own languages, to appoint their own officials, and to participate in their region's development. However, Khomeini refused their right to autonomy since it would jeopardize the unity of the state – an Islamic state (Fischer, 1980).

The country, he preached, needed to rid itself of "Westoxication." On November 4, 1979, the seizure of the U.S. Embassy in Tehran by a group of pro-Khomeini students symbolized to the world his new government's anti-imperialist and anti-Western sentiments (anti-imperialism was not only geared towards the U.S. but Israel and Russia as well).[17] Not only did the taking of the hostages send a message to Western governments, it sent a similarly alarming message to the Iranian public – both in Iran and abroad. For those in the United States, the taking of the hostages and the subsequent break in diplomatic relations put their future in jeopardy. The majority of Iranians in the West (particularly the United States which had the largest Iranian student population) were on student visas.[18]

Though the taking of the American hostages fueled Khomeini's anti-Western fervor, its overall effect of continued mobilization was limited in its ability to forge a "pure" Islamic state. Khomeini was desperate to unite the various political, ethnic, and religious factions. In addition, he had to balance national interests with his Islamic goals. Afrasiabi (1994) writes that "Khomeini's balancer role vis-à-vis the contesting elements of Iranian Revolution created a pattern of policy oscillation between these elements or 'combination' of two inseparable, inchoate sets of interests (and the ideological 'linkage groups' that pursued these interests) (p. 19)."

In the Midst of Islamization

On September 22, 1980, as Iran wrestled with political unrest, new policies, and general disorganization, Iran's neighboring country, Iraq, seized the opportunity to attack Iran. Baghdad was convinced that Iran could not retaliate since it was internationally isolated (due to the hostage crisis) and that there were internal post-revolutionary political conflicts. Paradoxically, Khomeini used the war as a means of mobilizing his new nation and advancing his Islamic state.[19] Neither able to offer jobs nor an education to Iranian youth, Khomeini instead directed them to the battlefields. He proclaimed it a holy war. More importantly, he was able to focus their attention away from the closing of institutions of higher learning that occurred just months prior to the war. What might otherwise have been a devastating war became a golden opportunity for Khomeini to solidify his rule.

The closing of the universities was the culmination of Khomeini's revolutionary rhetoric. He believed that all the misfortunes confronting mankind have their roots in the universities and that Iranian universities, in particular, were "westoxicated" and needed to reflect Islamic doctrines (Selhoun, 1983). Khomeini ordered the purging of dissident faculty and student bodies. The orders were carried out with force and aggression by Revolutionary Guards and armed gangs. The violence escalated on campuses as the

lists of dissidents grew. To justify its brutality, the
government emphasized that Islamization would not be
otherwise possible. By the middle of 1980, the
Revolutionary Council declared that the universities would
not open at the beginning of the next academic year, in
order to "prepare the foundation of an Islamic educational
system and to facilitate purges" (Mojab, 1991, p. 90). Only
months before the war with Iraq, the universities were
ordered closed (and they would remain closed for the
following three years) so that they could be Islamicized.

As in most social revolutions (e.g., Russia, China,
Cuba, Ethiopia, Nicaragua) in Iran, the institutions that
were deemed most powerful in spreading the revolutionary
ideals were its mediums of education and media (primarily
television and radio) (Ballantine, 1985; Parsons, 1966;
Wallace, 1961). Like earlier revolutionary leaders,
Khomeini too emphasized the importance of educating the
younger generation in accordance with the principles of the
Revolution. At the primary and secondary levels major
changes were introduced into the curricula: "The overriding
objectives were to stress values over knowledge, to make
education meet the needs of society, and to eradicate what
remained of the influence of the Pahlavi period" (Menashri,
1990, p. 227).

The Islamization process at higher levels of education
included rewriting textbooks, modifying curricula, and
purging faculty members. Faculty members were required
to take an examination concerning their academic
experience and political/religious ideology. Faculty
members' backgrounds were searched to determine if they
were loyal to the Islamic Republic. The government purged
approximately eight thousand faculty members – either
because of their relations with the Pahlavi regime or
because of their religious/political views. Iran's system of
higher education, already in dire need of trained educators,
was severely handicapped (Rucker, 1991).

Yet Khomeini's new Islamic government was willing to
sacrifice the quality of its system of education in order to
ensure its own survival. Afshar (1985) believes that there

was more to the closing of the universities than Islamization; that it was the new and fragile government's attempt at keeping the young and the educated from gathering in open forums and discussions. Since universities had historically been the grounds where political dissent was nurtured (such as those who opposed the Pahlavi regime), it was important to oppress activities within them (Afshar, 1985).

When postrevolutionary universities reopened in 1983, they had been entirely revamped.[20] Prayers were part of the daily ritual; Islamic dress was mandated for all faculty and students; classrooms were segregated between men and women[21] and all coeducational activities (such as sports) were strictly banned. Swimming was segregated, and women were no longer allowed to participate in public sports, such as basketball.

Most importantly, however, was the supplementation of an "ideological test" to the admissions process. The two-fold practice was to ensure the moral competency of the applicants. First, all applicants had to pass the written examination, then an investigation was made into the candidate's moral suitability to the Islamic Republic (Menashire, 1992). For example, investigators would interview the applicant's neighbors to determine a student's religiosity without questioning the credibility of the neighbor themselves (Entessar, 1984; Mojab, 1991). Those whom they unjustly accused had no recourse but to forgo their university ambitions.

The process of Islamization and the war had created a shortage of teachers, facilities, and resources (Rucker, 1991). When Khomeini declared that the hundreds of thousands of young men who had participated in the war were to be given priority in the admissions process, it exasperated those in an already strained system.

Despite the added rigors of entrance examinations, the lack of resources and trained faculty, the number of university hopefuls continued to dramatically increase. By the end of the decade and the war in 1989, 725,000 aspiring students took the examination; only 150,000 were accepted. Higher education continued to be viewed as the primary vehicle of advancement in the Iranian society; access to it also continued to be highly restrictive. Throughout this period, millions of Iranians continued to flee the country. First, there was the exodus of the ruling class or the elites. Second, there were the ethnic and religious minorities, who took Khomeini's promise of protection as rhetorical and instead sought protection outside of the country. As the Iran-Iraq war persisted and the universities remained closed, many middle-class Iranians, weary of the future the Islamic Republic of Iran had in store for them, also escaped. Lack of opportunities and freedom, the prospect of war and consequent war, along with the bleak economic market impacted all sectors of the society.

1988 – Present

Since 1988, Iran has changed significantly. The war with Iraq came to an end; a religious proclamation – *fatwa*[22] -- was declared against Salman Rushdie; Khomeini died and Ali Akbar Hashemi-Rafsanjani became president, followed by Khatami; Iran has been linked with terrorism abroad; corruption reached new heights, as did dissatisfaction with the regime. The economic situation of the majority of the populace has worsened since the installment of the Islamic Republic (Lautenschlager, 1986; Smith, 1984).

In July 1988, Iran accepted U.N. Security Council Resolution 598 – a cease-fire with Iraq. Throughout the war, the Iranian government had justified its failure to meet its revolutionary promises, such as economic and social justice. With the end of the war, there came an era of reconstructing the country. The Islamic government had more to do than rebuild the damages left from the war: it also had to build programs that would appease the populace hitherto compliant because of the war. Thousands of young men returned from war were ready to resume their lives –

either by getting an education or by joining the work force, neither of which the government could afford to provide. At a time when there were pressures on the Islamic Republic to revive its economic and social structure, the release of The Satanic Verses by Salman Rushdie was opportune. The government was able to use the book as a vehicle to, once again, rally support for its Islamic ideals and redirect youths' attention. Tehran Radio aired Khomeini's fatwa:

> The author of the book The Satanic Verses, which is contrary to Islam, the Prophet and the Koran, together with all those involved in its publication who were aware of its content, are hereby sentenced to death ...
> I call on zealous Muslims to execute them promptly on the spot they find them, so that no one else will dare to blasphemise (sic) Muslim sanctities. (cited in Simpson & Shubart, 1995, p. 157)

The Satanic Verses and its ensuing fatwa put in motion a series of terrorist activities outside and inside of Iran.[23] Moreover, it broke off diplomatic relations between Britain and Iran at a time when pragmatic moderates were working towards rapprochement with the West. It also continued to fuel the negative stereotypes of Iranians abroad, who were viewed as terrorists and zealots, as being medieval.

On June 4, 1989, three months after he issued his fatwa against Salman Rushdie, Khomeini died. Upon Khomeini's death, Ali Akbar Rafsanjani, a political moderate, the Speaker of the Majlis, commander-in-chief of the armed forces, and arguably the closest political figure to Khomeini, rose to the presidency. Rafsanjani immediately began repairing diplomatic relations broken with the European Community as a result of the Salman Rushdie death campaign. In June 1990, a devastating earthquake in northern Iran paved the way for Rafsnjani's appeal to the West. Despite criticism from radical and religious hardliners, Rafsanjani used the earthquake to illustrate the need for Iran to open up to the West.

With the end of the war with Iraq, and the succession of Rafsanjani to power, Iran began to tempt its nationals abroad to return to their homeland and help rebuild their country, offering men of military service age an opportunity to "purchase" their mandatory service time.[24] War veterans who had served their country resented this government incentive. There was decisively a national schism between those who had served their country and those who had not; those who had lived in Iran and those who had not. Two national identities had been created – one of those living in Iran and one for those in exile.

Despite the evident resentment within Iran for those who had resided outside the country, many Iranians did return to Iran, taking with them the Western culture and ideology they had acquired during their asylum. The Islamic Republic grappled with the benefits of returning nationals and the "polluting of minds" that the contact would bring about, but the former outweighed the latter, since Iran was in a desperate situation of "brain drain."

Iran's brain drain was severely felt within its institutions of higher education. In the early 1990s, Rafsanjani initiated the construction of a private university system called Azad University.[25] Azad centers sprung up in remote corners of Iran – often in nothing more than a decrepit building with no professors to conduct classes. Symbolically, however, it gave the impression to youth that the government was working to create a more encompassing system of higher education.

In August 1997, president Rafsanjani was succeeded by yet another political reformist, Mohammed Khatami, who won the presidential election by massive public support. Khatami received 20 million votes, while his conservative challenger, Ali Akbar Nateq-Nouri, only received seven million. The overwhelming message from the Iranian public to the ruling party was that Iran should become more moderate. The dominant themes that emerged from the election were that Iranians sought freedom of the press, a pluralistic political system, and more rights for women. In the summers of 2000 and 2003, Iranian students took to the streets again, chanting this time against the Islamic Republic. What is interesting about this group of protestors is that they are the offspring of the original revolutionaries. These are the youth who were educated in Khomeini's Islamicized system of education, a system that supposedly inculcated them with the ideals of the Islamic Revolution. Yet, these youth's complaints resounded the disgruntlement of an earlier generation: Iran's system of education continues to offer them no future hope.

CHAPTER TWO

Destinations

The 1979 Iranian Revolution was the impetus for the largest exodus of Iranians in its history. Some took refuge in neighboring countries, such as Turkey. Others made their way to Europe and Australia. But the majority of Iranians migrated to the United States. The largest concentration of émigré Iranians, those who settled in the United States, can be best described as evolving from having their "bags unpacked" to eventually realizing that "life goes on." This immigrant group is geographically dispersed, religiously and ethnically diverse, embodies a divisive national character, and adheres to circles that are demarcated by social class. Thus, the "Iranian immigrant community" and, more specifically, the "Iranian immigrant experience" include a complicated web of historical, political, and social relationships.

The Iranian Diaspora

Until the Iranian Revolution of 1979, the vast majority of those who left Iran were students. The Pahlavis' drive to industrialize Iran during the 1960s and 1970s created a need for educated and skilled labor (Fischer, 1980; Keddie, 1981; Zonis, 1971). Since Iranian universities could not meet the high rate of demand for higher education, Iranian students sought education in other countries, such as the United States, France, and Britain. These links that the Iranian students established with foreign universities would serve as the network through which many Iranians left during and after the Revolution.

The Iranian Revolution and subsequent political events (e.g., Iran-Iraq war) fueled the exodus of hundreds of thousands of Iranian refugees and exiles.[26] Among those fleeing the country in the late 1970s and the early 1980s were the political elite, religious minorities, and draft-age men who wanted to escape the Iran-Iraq war. During the 1980s, Iran was one of the top ten producing nations in terms of refugees (U.S. Committee for Refugees, 1989).

There is, however, no comprehensive data on the distribution of Iranians worldwide. For example, according to one source, there are over three and one half million Iranians worldwide (Iranian Christian International, 1996). Other sources approximate the Iranian Diaspora to be one or two million (World Survey, 1989). Bozorgmehr (1995, 1998) has culled data from national censuses in some countries that have settled Iranians and probably offers the most reliable data so far.

According to Bozorgmehr (1995), by 1990 there were approximately 637,500 Iranians in Germany, France, Sweden, Norway, USA, Canada, Australia, and Israel (see Table 4). Turkey, harboring one of the largest Iranian refugee/immigrant populations, is not included in this profile. Because of its proximity to Iran, Turkey hosts an estimated one million Iranians albeit that little is known about their status.[27]

Many Iranians settled in Israel where approximately 121,000 Iranians now reside. Pliskin (1987) breaks Iranian migration to Israel into four distinct timeframes: before 1948; 1948-1967; 1967-1977; and from 1978 on; with the median year of migration being 1958, not after the Iranian Revolution, as one would suspect.

Table 4: Distribution of Persian Diaspora in Selected Countries Circa 1990

Region and Country	Population of Iranians
North America	
United States	285,000
Canada	38,900
Europe	
West Germany	89,700
Sweden	39,000
Great Britain	32,300
France	7,000
Norway	5,900
Other	
Australia	13,900
Israel	121,300
Japan	4,500
Total	637,500

Source: Bozorgmehr,1995

Germany also attracted a large part of the Iranian migration, hosting approximately 90,000 Iranians. Germany, Norway, and Sweden have attracted many Iranians due to their lenient asylum policies. Norway, for example, hosts a relatively large Iranian Bahá'í community because they were granted humanitarian refugee status during the early 1980s (Kamalkhani, 1988).

According to the above data, the United States hosts more Iranians than any other nation. Just as there is controversy about the size of the Iranian Diaspora, there is disagreement about the number of Iranians living in the United States. The 1990 U.S. Census accounted only for 285,000 Iranians, including those born in Iran and with Iranian ancestry and the 2000 U.S. Census estimated the number of Iranian-Americans to be 338,000.[28] The Iranian community has continued to refute Census figures approximating the size of their community. The Iranian Studies Group (ISG), founded in 2002 by a group of MIT Ph.D. students has compiled a population estimate of 691,000 Iranian-Americans. The Interest Section of the Islamic Republic of Iran in Washington DC claims that 1,300,000 individual Iranians living in the United States have processed passports with their office.

U.S. Migration

Iranian migration to the United States was a post-World War II phenomenon, characterized by two distinct waves.[29] Though the original intent of both waves of immigrants, according to the literature, was not to reside in the United States permanently, throughout the 1980s, as Iran destabilized economically, an overwhelming number of Iranians reluctantly established permanent U.S. residency.

The first postwar group of Iranians migrated primarily for educational reasons. During the early 1970s, in the midst of a rapidly expanding economy, Iran lacked the educational infrastructure to support its economic growth. Consequently, both the private sector and the government of Iran financed the education of many of its nationals in foreign countries. Their preferred destination was the United States. Between 1950 and 1978, an annual average of 1,515 immigrants and 17,001 non-immigrants[30] entered the United States (Sabagh & Bozorgmehr, 1987). Also see Table 5 below.

While members of the first wave (i.e., students) typically migrated alone, many members of the second wave, those escaping political and religious persecution, generally migrated in family units (Sabagh & Bozorgmehr, 1987). For the newly arrived second wave of Iranians, family ties often influenced where they settled in the United States and, ultimately, the experiences of their children.

Table 5: Iranian Immigrants and Non-Immigrants Admitted to the United States, 1950-1980.

Year	Immigrants Admitted	Nonimmigrants Admitted
1950	245	644
1955	219	1113
1960	429	3705
1965	804	5954
1970	1825	14475
1975	2337	35088
1979	8476	65813
1980	10410	NA
Annual Averages		
1950-1977	1,515	17,001
1978-1980	8,249	112,205

Source: Immigration and Naturalization Service (1958-1977, 1978-1980).

The U.S. Iranian Population: Unpacked Bags[31]

Iranians who migrated to the United States during the 1979 revolutionary period left a country in political turmoil and entered an antagonistic host society. Americans saw Iranian immigrants as extensions of the new Islamic Republic government under Ayatollah Ruhollah Khomeini who had instigated the capture of fifty-two American hostages and held them for fourteen months. The ordeal was heavily publicized as "the hostage crisis" by the U.S. government and media. Political analysts linked the hostage crisis directly to the United States experience in Vietnam. Joel Fleishman, at the time director of the Institute of Policy Sciences and Public Affairs at Duke University, stated, "This [hostage crisis] really reached way down to our subconscious. America had always been the great, powerful nation. We stood for things we admire; we were able to get things done; we'd never lost a war. Now, we've not only lost a war, we're losing the peace" (Roberts, 1980, p. 2). For some the hostage crisis had become the watershed event of American politics; debates between presidential candidates Ronald Reagan and Jimmy Carter during the 1980 presidential elections were centered on this national dilemma. Americans' apprehension about rising inflation, interest rates, home prices, crime rates, nuclear proliferation, immigrants, poverty, preserving the environment, and affording college for their children were all wrapped up in one single unifying national problem: the hostage crisis. This national crisis created fear among the American public that the U.S. position, or perceived position, of world leadership was seriously deteriorating. In this sociopolitical context, reprisals against Iranians living in the United States were a natural extension. Among Americans, the prevalent image of Iranians was violent, flag-burning Islamic zealots. Ironically, that image was incongruent with the profile of those Iranians who had elected to migrate to the United States, many of whom fled because of the increasing Islamic zeal in Iran. Moreover, the US-Iranian population is by far more heterogeneous, in terms of religious and ethnic diversity, than Iran's generally homogeneous population.

Those Iranians who fled the Islamic Revolution in the years immediately following 1979 were most likely to be skilled and educated: members of the country's elite class, intellectuals, religious minorities, and secular Muslims. In 1980, 40 percent of them held a bachelor's degree or an advanced degree – twice the rate among all other foreign-born immigrants arriving between 1970 and 1980 and two and a half times that among the native-born U.S. population (Bozorgmehr, Sabagh, & Der-Martirosian, 1993). The overall characteristic of this immigrant group was that they had an astonishing number of "high-status immigrants." Not only did this characteristic make them unlike other post-1965 immigrants who came to the United States with lower levels of education and primarily for economic reasons; it also set them apart from other refugees. Iranians were unlike other recent refugees who tended to be socioeconomically disadvantaged.

The departure of Iranians from their homeland has been likened to that of refugees from Cuba and Vietnam (Sabagh & Bozorgmehr, 1987). Webster dictionary defines a "refugee" as a person who flees his home or country to seek refuge elsewhere, as in a time of war, or political or religious persecution. This definition accurately describes the majority of Iranians who arrived in the United States after the Iranian Revolution. Yet, post-revolutionary Iranians were never officially recognized by the United States as refugees because of the circumstances between the two countries during the late 1970s. Since they were never categorically granted refugee status, they never benefited from its associated refugee benefits/rights.

Another significant aspect of Iranian migration to the United States is that those who arrived during or after the Revolution had a strong desire to return to Iran. They regarded life in the United States as temporary.[32] Naficy (1991) describes how this longing to return to their homeland, "a longing that is intensified by the inability of many to return" (p. 288), is central to understanding the Iranian immigrant experience. He continues, "Exile is a contentious state, and the feelings of community and unification produced by these fetishes and souvenirs are disrupted by the dilemmas of hesitation, ambivalence, and indeterminacy, which mark all exiles" (p. 290). His description of the Iranian refugee/exile experience provides a strong basis for understanding the nature of the Iranian community that has since evolved. That is, Iranians had left a politically fractured country and entered a hostile host society. Feeling at odds with their host society, they have considered their stay as temporary and have not been able to form a coherent community. In the late 1980s, a survey of Iranians in the Los Angeles area revealed that Iranians felt they were discriminated against when it came to finding jobs, and were subjected to threats and violence. The following quotes (see Bozorgmehr, 2000, p. 172) illustrate the nature of the "hostility" Iranians felt:

> With seven years of professional experience and education I received no responses from any companies to which I was sending my resumé. Then I changed my name from Mohammad to Mike in my resume and immediately got four responses, including one from a company that had not responded to Mohammad.

> My wife and children were insulted at work and in school. They also insulted us so much in our apartment building that we had to move out of there. They called us 'dirty Iranians.'

> Anti-Iranian slogans were written on the walls of my workplace. One day I received a bomb threat at my workplace.

I should note, however, that these sentiments were felt in the years during and immediately following the hostage crisis. As Bozorgmehr (2000) notes, "whereas about a quarter of respondents reported serious cases of discrimination during the hostage crisis, only about one-tenth did so for the period just prior to the survey in 1987-88" (p. 170).

Because of the intense negativity to which Iranians felt subjected in the early 1980s, most did not want to draw attention to themselves – neither from Americans, nor from

their co-nationals. They did not want the attention of
Americans because of the political tensions between the
two countries; and they did not want the attention of co-
nationals because the traditional social lines – class,
ethnicity, and religion – had been blurred in their new host
society. Most Iranians, as a result, were apprehensive about
making contact with fellow Iranians. Political factionalism,
as well as extreme heterogeneity in terms of religion and
ethnicity (see "Religious-ethnic Diversity" below), have
been cited as reasons for lack of in-group cohesion among
Iranians (Bozorgmehr, 1993, 2000; Hoffman, 1988).
As a result, Iranians became invisible, silent – not only
to the American public but also among themselves. A
representative from California's Coalition for Immigrant
Rights characterized this immigrant community as a "silent
community" (Parsons, 1988). Hoffman (1988) quotes an
Iranian professional as saying,

> We are a quiet minority, a successful minority,
> unlike other minorities. We don't want to be
> thought of as just another bunch of immigrants (p.
> 166).

Recently, realizing the socio-political implications of
their "silence" Iranians have chartered organizations that
address these issues of discrimination. Similar to the goals
of the American Arab Antidiscrimination Council or the
Anti-Defamation League, for example, the Persian Watch
Cat: Iranian American Anti-Discrimination Center is
petitioning the incoming Bush administration against
discriminatory acts to Iranian-Americans.[33]
Whether real or perceived, Iranian sentiments of felt
hostility needs to be placed in the American context where
"every new wave of immigration reactivates an eternal
question: How do the 'new' immigrants measure up to the
'old'"(Suárez-Orozco, 2000, p. 7)? Most newly arrived
immigrant groups throughout this country's history have
felt shunned upon arrival, and the experience of Iranians is

certainly not unique to America's history. Cubans and Nicaraguans, for example, were two other groups who fled their country's revolutions and were initially unfavorably treated by the American public (Bozorgmehr, 2000). The "American hostility" then must taken into account America's paradoxical relationship with immigrants, where as Suárez-Orozco (2000) states, "immigration is at once history and destiny" (p.7). The felt hostility, however, is at the core of understanding the Iranian immigrant experience.

Life Goes On in America

More than ten years after the Iranian Revolution, the 1990 U.S. Census (see Table 6) provided a profile of how Iranian immigrants began establishing themselves. It showed that most first-generation Iranian immigrants were educationally and economically on a par with the average native-born White U.S. citizen. Eighty percent of first-generation Iranian immigrants were employed and 40 percent held upper-level, white-collar jobs (U.S. Bureau of Census, 1993). Over 50 percent of those twenty-five and older held bachelor's degrees, making them the third most highly educated immigrant group, after Indians and Taiwanese (U.S. Bureau of Census, 1993). Moreover, they had a 21 percent rate of self-employment – one of the highest among immigrants – in the fields of dentistry and medicine (U.S. Bureau of Census, 1993). Rates of homeownership also reveal that their high socioeconomic status enabled them to move into middle- and upper-class neighborhoods.

Economic assimilation into American society, combined with the impossibility of returning to their homeland, changed the Iranian immigrant mentality. Gradually, these immigrants reconciled themselves to permanent U.S. residency. By 1996, nearly a quarter of the Iranian population in this country was under eighteen (Ansari, 1997; Bozorgmehr, Der-Martirosian, & Sabagh, 1996): a second generation was emerging.[34] This showed that as first generation Iranians reared a new generation in this country, they began to shed themselves as transients. Rather, they slowly accepted the permanence of their U.S. residency.

Table 6: Educational Attainment, Median Household Incomes and Poverty Rates, 1990

Country of Birth	Total	Education		Income	
		% complete d 4 years of college or More (25 years or older)	% High School Graduate (25 years or older)	Median House- hold Income $	Poverty Rate
Native-Born	228,942,557	20.3	77.0	30,176	12.7
Foreign-Born	19,767,316	20.4	58.8	28,314	18.2
Iranian immigrant	210,941	50.6	86.7	35,836	15.7

Source: U.S. Bureau of Census, The Foreign-Born Population in the United States, CP-3-1, Washington, D.C.: U.S. Department of Commerce, July 1993, tables 1, 3, and 5.

With the exception of Iranians in the Los Angeles area,[35] the U.S. Iranian community is distributed widely. One could argue that Iranians' lack of proximity to co-nationals is evidence that they have been able to rapidly integrate themselves into the American middle class. And others contend that their integration is merely structural, not cultural[36] (Ansari, 1992; Bozorgmehr & Sabagh, 1988; Chaichian, 1997; Hoffman, 1988, 1989; Naficy, 1993). That is, Iranians have taken advantage of the avenues through which they can achieve successful economic status in the United States, but they have resisted assimilating into the American social culture.

The issue of assimilation by Iranians has been the focus of much research and speculation among the Iranian scholarly community, particularly as it relates to intergenerational conflict (Ansari, 1992; Ghaffarian, 1987; Mashayekhi, 1992; Mahdi, 1998; Naficy, 1991, 1993). At the center of the discussion rests concerns about how the Iranian culture is being preserved/maintained for future generations. For instance, many Iranian scholars have described how first-generation Iranian immigrants have tried to teach and promote their home culture to their children. Ansari (1992) explains that as they resigned themselves to the permanence of their exile, immigrants began "to create their own communal structure" as a way of passing on their culture to the next generation of Iranians (p. 132). Naficy (1993) proposes that Los Angeles-originated Iranian television and pop music have served as media of cultural preservation for Iranians. Others assert that cultural associations, Farsi language programs, community events, community centers, Farsi media, and the Iranian Yellow Page Directory[37] are elements of the Iranian community in exile. In the Los Angeles area, Iranian parent organizations financially support efforts that are adding Farsi to school curricula (Mitchell, 1999).

However, Mahdi (1998) believes that the desire of first-generation Iranians to preserve their national identity conflicts with the realities of their non-territorial community in the United States: "Iranians in the United States are a diverse demographic and sociocultural population who have left their home country under various circumstances, for different reasons, and with dissimilar goals and objectives" (p. 79). It is this diversity among Iranians that has kept them divided in Diaspora and complicates any attempt at defining characteristics of an Iranian culture. Thus, without similar national goals and objectives, this disparate community will find it difficult to sustain itself culturally.

Is there an Iranian community in the United States or, as Mahdi argues, are there too many "disparate" factors within this community to join them? In the next sections, I will discuss three factors – besides their geographic dispersion -- that work against the formation of an Iranian community: religious-ethnic diversity, Iranian national character, and social class.

Religious-Ethnic Diversity

The most salient divide among Iranians in this country is their lack of internal cohesiveness. That is, Iranians are highly diverse in terms of religious-ethnicity (major subgroups include Shi'i Muslims, Armenians, Assyrian Christians, Jews, Bahá'ís, Kurds, and Zorastrians).[38] These religious-ethnic groups may have comprised only a small percentage of Iran's total population, but it is precisely these groups that fled the Iranian Revolution and as such they represent a larger portion of the overall Iranian community in the United States. This religious-ethnic diversity among Iranians has recently been referred to in the sociological literature as internal ethnicity, "the presence of ethnic groups within an immigrant group" (Bozorgmehr, Sabagh, & Der-Martirosian, 1993, p.59).[39] The schisms between these subgroups, combined with a national character (discussed below) underscore these divisions and is at the core of understanding this immigrant "community," or lack thereof.

In this section, I briefly describe six religious and ethnic groups: Muslims, Jews, Armenians, Bahá'ís, Zoroastrians, and Kurds. I do not discuss the remaining groups – Assyrians, Turks, and Baluchis – since there is little clear data about these sub-communities in the United States.

I would like to point out that a description of each religious and ethnic category is further complicated by additional variations within each group. For instance, though the majority of Iranian Muslims are Shiites (as opposed to Sunni), there is a wide range of definitions as to who may consider themselves a "Muslim." The majority of Iranian immigrants who fled Iran's Islamic Republic tended to be secular. Their notion of Islam is very different from that of devout Muslims (as discussed below).

Muslims

Islam in the Iranian-American community is wrought with political overtones.[40] Only a few hundred Iranian Americans pledge their allegiance to the Islamic Republic; the remainder of the Iranian Muslim community fled to the United States to disavow themselves from the Islamic regime (Haddad & Smith, 1994). These Iranian immigrants typically came from the more Westernized, secular stratum of the Iranian society – "a class that in the Pahlavi era was not religiously observant" (Hermansen, 1994, p. 187). For these Iranians, the Islamic Revolution forced them away from their comfortable homes and lifestyles, their professions, family, and friends, and instead placed them in a society that perceived Islam as violent and medieval -- a negative image with financial and emotional costs.

Most Iranians in the United States who do in fact refer to themselves as Muslims do not so much observe the tenets of the religion but rather perform cultural customs and traditions associated with Islam. For example, they hold weddings, funerals, and holidays in accordance with Islam, but do not attend daily worship.

Jews

Iranian Jews consider themselves to be the true Iranians. Some trace their roots back to 2,700 years ago when the Persian king Cyrus the Great took control of Palestine and freed its enslaved Jewish population. The biblical book of Esther describes Jewish life in Persia and the basis of Purim, a festive Jewish holiday.[41] The Jewish community has also been traced back to 586 BCE, to the destruction of the first Temple by Nebuchadnezzar.

Pliskin (1987) describes the history of Iranian Jews by two major themes: social insecurity and cultural perseverance. She states:

The insecurity that minorities suffered in Iran due to their submission to the domination of the Shi'ite majority was time and again intensified by religious riots.... The insecurity minorities have experienced historically concerns the powerlessness and instability of living in a situation where the clergy and the secular leaders were at odds with one another, and the minorities were the people played with in their struggles for power. The riots, coupled with the debasing religiously inspired Covenant of Omar, put all religious minorities, not just Jews, in humiliating positions. The alleviation of the abject status by the Pahlavi dynasty only further elicited anti-Jewish sentiment when Israel came into existence. Some Jews coped with this new anti-Jewishness by moving to Israel, whereas others, less influenced by the occasional anti-Jewish slurs and demonstrations, remained in Iran as full-fledged Iranians. (p. 34)

The upheavals of the Iranian Revolution, however, forced the majority of the Iranian Jewish population to other countries. Major settlement areas in the United States are Los Angeles, New York, Chicago, and San Francisco. Iranian Jews do not generally affiliate themselves with American Jewish groups. Most American Jews are of Ashkenazic or Sephardic descent; the former are originally from Eastern or Central Europe, while the latter are a branch of Mediterranean Judaism. Iranian Jews are identified as Mizrahi or Middle Eastern Jews, further complicating the intersection of their Jewish identity in relation to the dominant Jewish branches (Dallalfar, 1999). The differentiation is summed up in a divide along religious, linguistic, and cultural differences among Iranian and American Jews. Feher (1998) believes that this differentiation between American and Iranian Jews best characterizes the Jewish Iranian immigrant experience in the United States – segregation not integration.

Iranian Jews, like other Iranians, initially thought of their stay in the United States as temporary. As the years passed, they too, accepted the permanence of their residency. Among Iranian Jews, however, this decision has had broader implications. Their identities need to be balanced along three lines – Iranian, Jewish, and American – causing a "tricultural conflict" (Feher, 1998, p. 79). Identities are further confounded within the Iranian-Jewish community, particularly for those in New York. There are approximately four thousand Mashadi Jews living in Great Neck, New York, who distinctly set themselves apart from the larger Iranian Jewish community. Mashad, a trading outpost in Northeastern Iran, forced its Jewish community to convert to Islam in 1839 or face execution; they chose to go underground. The Mashadi Jewish community's clandestine practices continued until 1925 when Reza Shah lifted the prohibition. Based on observation and numerous interviews, Ungar (1995) describes this community:

> The Mashadi are surely among America's strongest believers in group identity and what have come to be known in modern American politics as "family values." Divorce is almost unheard of, and they tend to be very conservative on social issues, adamantly opposed to abortion and worried over the general permissiveness in modern society. Yet the Mashadi generally shy away from involvement in the larger society's institutions and politics. Some attribute this to their having been outsiders in Iran, an experience that left them believing it safer not to be noticed…. They do business primarily with each other. (p. 312)

Mashadis in the U.S. have their own internal organization, composed of thirty to fifty men who oversee all community affairs, including the building of a new synagogue, Hebrew School, and Mashadi Jewish Center of Great Neck. I should also note that the Iranian Jewish community is diverse and the Mashadi Jews are not representative of the entire Jewish community in the States.

Armenians

Armenians were recognized as an official religious minority under Iran's 1906 constitution. Although some Armenians may have encountered individual prejudice in Iran, they have not been subjected to state-sanctioned persecution. During the twentieth century, they have been an integral part of the economic and social life of Tehran and Esfehan – two centers with the greatest number of Armenian inhabitants. Armenians achieved a relatively high standard of living and maintained a large number of parochial primary and secondary schools (though often at odds with the Islamic Republic over their governance). Their migration to the United States can be attributed to educational and economic reasons more than to religious persecution.

Iranian Armenians arrived in the United States with substantial knowledge of Western culture and business practice due to their Westernized lives under the Shah. Their migration began just after World War II when a small community of Armenians established itself in Glendale, California, to take advantage of economic and educational opportunities. Glendale, a predominantly White, conservative, middle-class community, now harbors one of the largest Iranian Armenian communities in the United States. Though there are Armenians of other origins (e.g., Lebanon, Russia), Iranian Armenians are generally more economically successful than Armenians from other nations (Bozorgmehr, et al., 1996). Whether for economic or social reasons, Iranian Armenians consider themselves different than other Armenians (Kelley, 1993).

Bahá'ís

Nearly half of the Iranian Bahá'í community lives in
Southern California. The community of five to six thousand
people values peace and equality of race, class, and gender;
alcohol and premarital sex are forbidden. Despite their
universal tolerance ideals, they have had their own share of
tenuous relations within the Iranian community and with
the broader American Bahá'í community.

The Bahá'ís have a long history of antagonism with
Muslims. The Bahá'í faith emerged as a messianic
movement in 1844, after the Islamic revelation. Unlike
Judaism and Christianity, which are both accepted by
Muslims as tracing a lineage to the prophet Mohammed,
the Bahá'í faith is considered heresy. Thus, Bahá'í
followers have endured a long history of persecution in
Iran. Those outside the faith typically distrust the Bahá'í
community.

The American Bahá'í community is generally of
middle- and working-class backgrounds, and many are
African American, while Iranian Bahá'ís, like other Iranian
immigrants, were generally more affluent (Kelly, 1993).
Race and class have worked as segregating agents between
the American and the Iranian Bahá'í communities. Kelly
(1993) also discusses how their differing histories have
kept the two communities at bay:

> When the Iranians first began arriving, many local
> Bahá'ís expected these newcomers from the birth
> place of the faith to be tempered experts with keen
> insights into the Bahá'í religion. In this regard, the
> Americans were sometimes sorely disappointed.
> Most Iranians were Bahá'ís by birth and did not
> exhibit the zeal of the American converts. Some
> Persians were more lax than Americans in
> observing prohibitions against alcohol and formal
> marriage regulations. Those from Iran were mostly
> second-,third-, and fourth-generation Bah'is....
> American Bahá'ís, in contrast, tend to be activists.

As recent converts, they are often the only family members to accept the faith.... American Bahá'ís typically perceive themselves as a dynamically expanding community governed by rules and laws rather than as a passive sacred community governed by God. (pp.130 - 31)

Zoroastrians

Zoroastrianism initially developed in Iran during the seventh century BCE, and lasted until the imposition of Islam by the Arabs in seventh century A.D. After Iran's incorporation into the Islamic empire, the majority of its population was gradually converted from Zoroastrianism to Islam.

During the mid-nineteenth century, Zoroastrians experienced considerable prejudice. As a result, several thousand Zoroastrians emigrated from Iran to British-ruled India to improve their economic and social status. This group, known as Parsis, is distinguished from Iranian Zoroastrians. It was not until the rule of the Pahlavis that the status of Zoroastrians was elevated to a more respected position in the Iranian society. Today, like Christians and Jews, the Zoroastrians are recognized as an official religious minority under the Iranian Constitution of 1979. As with the Armenians, their migration to the United States has been driven by economic, rather than religious, reasons.

Approximately three thousand Zoroastrians live in the United States – concentrated in New York, San Francisco, Chicago, and Los Angeles. There are two Iranian Zoroastrian centers – one located in San Francisco and the other in New York, though one-third of the Iranian-Zoroastrians live in Southern California.[42]

Zoroastrians have a historic commitment to education that is reflected, like other Iranians, in their high levels of educational attainment. They are discreet about their faith and do not proselytize to gain new members.[43]

Kurds

It is difficult to approximate the Kurdish population – either worldwide or in the United States. Since there is no legitimate census of this ethnic group in any of these countries, figures of this community are disputed between political activists and scholars (Kelley, 1993). Their origins are rooted in four countries in the Middle East: Iran, Iraq, Turkey, and Syria. It is the strategic geographic location of Kurdistan that has kept any of these four countries from allowing the Kurds to establish autonomy. Kurdish Iranians have resented the ethnic oppression of their peoples, such as not being able to publish books that narrate the history of their people. In the United States, they often prefer to identify themselves as Kurds (their ethnicity) rather than Iranians (their national origin).

The internal diversity among Iranians fragments the notion of a unified or a singular Iranian community, given that each sub-community conforms to its own sets of customs, traditions, and values. Below I discuss how the Iranian "national character," rather than being a binding factor, further exacerbates the splintering among these subgroups.

The Iranian "National" Character

Mead (1962) defined "national character" as "a group of persons with a shared social tradition whose culture is selected because they are the citizens or subjects – the 'nationals' – of a sovereign political state" (p. 396). Given the wide range of regional, religious, linguistic, cultural, and socioeconomic differences among Iranians, such a single profile seems counterintuitive. Yet, it is plausible to believe that a thread of shared characteristic must also exist amongst people who have shared a common land.

Nearly all the scholarly work relating to the Iranian national character has been written by Westerners (Bateson, 1979; Beeman, 1976; Binder, 1963; Hass, 1946; James, 1972; Pliskin, 1987; Westwood, 1965). The common traits cited by these scholars are based on Iran's long history of conquest by autocratic regimes. In a context of oppressive rule, Iranians learned to display an "appropriate" outer behavior in the social arena and to conceal their own personal inner behavior, for the private realm. Such behavior among Iranians is best explained by two concepts: the *birun* (outer) and *andarun* (inner) of an individual's physical and mental state. That is, what one reveals on the outside is markedly different from what lies within an individual. Understanding the concept of inner/outer is at the core of the traits that have been identified as being the national Iranian character. Bateson (1979; also see Westwood, 1965) discusses the roots of the inner/outer schism among Iranians.

It seems probable that the thematic understanding of the relationship between inner and outer in Iranian culture has interacted throughout history with autocratic forms of government that force the concealment of individual convictions and the elaboration of external forms; yet the interest in hidden purity as expressed in these many different areas, seems too basic to be an artifact of a form of government or a tradition of police surveillance. The cultivated consciousness of dissonance between inner and outer, in which influences from society are the source of evil and corruption, seems to transcend political externals, and yet it cannot but influence political developments. (p. 132)

As a result of this inner/outer distinction, Iranians, as observed by Westerners, are seen as deceptive, mistrustful, clever/wily, insecure, and emotional. While each of these characteristics can be debated,[44] Iranian scholars (Ansari, 1977; Chaichian, 1997; Feher, 1998, Pliskin, 1987) have repeatedly cited one feature –mistrust – as endemic to Iranian immigrants.

The combination of an internal diversity and a divisive national character are further confounded by a mentality that is highly conscientious of social class.

Social Class

Middle Eastern societies are, like most societies, socially hierarchical (Rosen, 1979). Social relationships/interactions are dependent on one's economic class. One avenue by which social mobility can be obtained is through earning higher education credentials (Beeman, 1976; Zonis, 1971). In a hierarchical society such as Iran, where social mobility is possible and people of various statuses interact, communication patterns reinforce the general social structure (Pliskin, 1987). For example, language – both verbal and nonverbal – is one indicator of social class among Iranians.

The structure of verbal Farsi denotes distance and respect to those of higher status. For example, the verb "to come" (*amadan*) is used differently to relate status. When one is talking about someone of much higher status than oneself, one uses a compounded verb form that means, literally, "to bring your honor" (*tashrif avardan*) (Pliskin, 1987).

One form of both verbal and nonverbal behavior that best illustrates how social status is observed among Iranians is the cultural decorum of *ta'arof*, which Beeman (1976a) defines as "the active, ritualized realization of differential status in interaction. It underscores and preserves the integrity of culturally defined status roles as it is carried out in the life of every Iranian every day in thousands of different ways" (p. 132). Beeman's (1976b) anthropological linguistic interpretation of this phenomenon provides a more detailed interpretation:

> Every time tea is offered to a group, every time a group of persons wish to proceed through the one door, every time friends meet on the street, every time guests proceed to the dinner table at a party,

the constant unceasing reutilization of the assessment of the climate of relative status occurs and reoccurs. It is this more than any other actor which gives social life in Iran its unique flavor compared to other oriental societies. The fact that status is relative for individuals in different interaction situations, and the fact that as a result of this relativity rights and obligations shift constantly with changes in one's social environment, make these constant social gestures important tools in every day social relations. (p. 312)

Pliskin's (1987) interpretation is as follows:

Guests ritually refuse the food several times while the host ritually presents the offerings until the guests take something. Other forms of *ta'arof* consist of seating the high status guest at the head of the room; jockeying for positions of status, especially lower status, in leaving a room in which the high-status person leaves the door first; asking a long series of questions about various members of a person's family when meeting a person in the street or when talking on the telephone before proceeding to transact business; seeing someone in the street and inviting him or her to one's house for tea, both knowing full well that the invitation is simply a formality; making offers to people which they have to refuse, such as telling someone who admires an article of clothing that she can take it as a present (*pishkesh*). (p. 53; also see Bateson, 1979)

Verbal and nonverbal behavior, such as the ritual of *ta'arof*, is an indication that Iranians are conscience of social class. This tendency also acts as a disruptive factor within the Iranian community.

Second-Generation Iranians

It is not surprising that second-generation Iranian youth, coming to terms with their sense of being are grappling with often-contradictory aspects of their identity. A recent surge of Iranian-American biographies recounts lives between two very different cultures (see Asayesh, 1999; Bahrampour, 1999; Karim & Khorrami, 1999; Rachlin, 1995). The common theme among these books is the Iranian community's struggle to understand what it means to be an Iranian in America.

Mahdi (1998) examines the construction of identity among second-generation Iranians -- the only study that has thus far broached this topic. Among his diverse religious-ethnic sample of 1.5 and second-generation Iranians, he found that their perceptions of their sense of being an Iranian are often unclear: "Second-generation Iranians have shown a strong interest in maintaining a sense of their ancestral roots and culture. However, such a desire is predicated on an Americanized understanding of Iranian culture and conditioned by the characteristics of the American multicultural society" (p. 94).

Putting Down Roots

The educational experiences of second-generation Iranians have been shaped within a specific historical, political, and social context. These students grew up in the aftermath of a failed U.S.-Iran relationship. The U.S. media image cast "Iranians" in extreme terms -- as both terrorists and filthy rich. Immigration scholars commonly describe this immigrant group as one that continues to wait for an eventual return -- that their stay in the U.S. is temporary, a sojourn rather than permanent migration. What is missing from these media and scholarly portrayals is the spectrum of experiences of second-generation Iranians, and that their "home" has now long been established here. The below quote of a Jewish female student is a preview of what my study unveils:

I asked my dad once if he would want to go back but he didn't really answer. Because we have our life here, he has his business here, I know that he would never want to move back there. Just because we're settled so well here. We're well off here.

Although the new generation continues to feel the pull of their homeland, they explain that the United States is now their home. One Armenian male participant captures the disappearance of their parents' and grandparents' homeland:

Iran, at least for my family, isn't looked upon as it used to be. Like it's now something in the past. Because I remember when I was younger it was discussed more and it was like a lot more reference to it. Like now the references are gone. It used to be that they would bring things up more in the past. Now they don't bring it up. Like things they did in Iran or happened in Iran. Now, it's more like that's past us and it's more like what's happening in Armenia now. At first it was a nice mix of Armenia and Iran but now it's only what's happening in Armenia. And because we know so few people in Iran that it's even less discussed in the family household. It seems that as the years go by the people who were in my family from Iran get more distanced from the country, you know?

For some, like Bahá'ís and Jewish Iranians, who fled to escape persecution in Iran, the prospect of eventually returning was even more remote. One Jewish-Iranian female said that in her high school junior year she partook in a program called the "March of the Living," which included a trip to Israel and to a holocaust site. In writing a college essay she had an experience analogous to that of her parents leaving Iran:

When I was writing my essay I realized that I was paralyzed. It was very close to the experience my parents had when they were leaving Iran. ... I was putting myself in the situation of my parents like they escaped illegally .... As a Jewish person I feel I can't go back to Iran. I don't want to go to Iran.

And a male Iranian Bahá'í captures how his family sees the United States as their home:

One time I asked my father, don't you miss Iran, don't you want to go back? and he said, well, really everything that I enjoy comes from Iran, I enjoy here. I enjoy the language. I enjoy the food. I enjoy the people; who I was in pretty close contact [with], they've all pretty much left.... Home is here.

CHAPTER THREE

An Emerging Generation

The design of this project began with two preliminary steps. First, I had several informal interviews with teachers in Los Angeles area schools that had a substantial number of second-generation Iranian students. This gave me a glimpse, from the perspective of teachers, of what sort of educational experiences these students have had in high school. Second, I held an informal focus group with first-generation Iranian parents of college students. This gathering helped me understand the perspective of parents: how they view the lives, and in particular the education, of their children.

Epistemological and Methodological Frameworks

In the broadest sense, my method of research is based on naturalistic inquiry in that it considers the relationship between individuals' experience and the society in which they live. I sought to link the broad historical, political, and social context of Iranians to the individual experiences of their second-generation members living in the United States. My role as a researcher who shares the same national background as her subjects, and as a mother raising an Iranian-American child intertwined me in the lives of my participants. I was the co-constructor of their narratives in the way I asked the questions and in my interpretation of their experiences. In that sense, my approach to this study is influenced by the interpretive tradition in the social sciences. Westkott (1990) observes the nature of interpretive approach in research:

> [S]ocial knowledge is always interpreted within historical contexts, and that truths are, therefore, historical rather than abstract, and contingent rather than categorical. The interpretive approach also assumes that these historical truths are grasped not by attempting to eliminate subjectivity but through the intersubjectivity of meaning of subject and object. This intersubjectivity does not mean the identity of subject and object, but rather their dialectical relationship. Thus the questions that the investigator asks of the object of knowledge grow out of her own concerns and experiences. The answers that she may discover emerge not only from the ways that the objects of knowledge confirm and expand these experiences, but also from the ways that they oppose or remain silent about them. Hence, the intersubjectivity of meaning takes the form of dialogue from which knowledge is an unpredictable emergent rather than a controlled outcome. (pp. 61-62)

Using the interpretive frame of reference, the necessary method of data collection was in-depth interviews. I followed an interview protocol during my interviews, but the discussion that ensued was typically more like what Kahn and Cannell (1957) describe as a "conversation with a purpose" (p. 149).

My aim in this study was to expand our conceptual understanding of only one aspect of the Iranian community in the United States (Eisner, 1991). I make no claim of external generalizability to Iranian undergraduate students who attend colleges and universities outside New England (Maxwell, 1996). The educational experiences of my subjects are very likely to be different from those students who attend schools in California, where there is a large Iranian population.

Researcher Role Management: Reflexivity, Entry, and Ethics

Many researchers before me have commented on the difficulty of studying this community -- that researchers are viewed with a high degree of distrust and suspicion, that their conception of a researcher is someone who is nosy and "meddlesome" (see Ansari, 1977). Khalili (1998) captures the essence of researching the Iranian-American community:

The culture of distrust and paranoia, so carefully cultivated by both the Pahlavi regime and the Islamic Republic as a means of creating a self-policing environment, continues to haunt us in the way we approach and interact with one another in exile. We need to know each other's political affiliations before we consider what the other says as credible; we subconsciously find ourselves on the brink of "being reported." (p. 12)

My experience was in line with those of past researchers and was perhaps more conflicted because of the ambiguities surrounding my own role/identity as an Iranian. This point warrants a detailed explanation.

Researcher Reflexivity

One overriding factor at the center of this research was my relationship with my interviewees and my interpretation of their narratives. It was a dynamic that rested on my own Iranian-American identity – as both someone who grew up in the United States and as one who is now rearing children who can also be considered "second-generation Iranians."

My family migrated during the first wave of migration (see chapter three) which was primarily comprised of students, not family units. There were many Iranian college students at that time, but Iranian families, as a unit, rarely migrated during this first wave. I went to high school in a small town in Rhode Island where in my graduating high school senior class there were only two minorities. There was an African-American and myself. I was administratively referred to as the "foreigner." In the fall of 1979, during the eve of the hostage crisis, I was a senior in high school taking extra credits at the University of Rhode Island. It was a politically tense time for being an Iranian on an American college campus at that time. Iranian students were factionalized – some came to campus dressed in Islamic garb to demonstrate their allegiance to Khomeini; others vehemently advocated for the continued reign of the Pahlavi regime. The University newspaper was filled with editorials condemning Iranian students and asking for their departure from the University. Since I had not grown up with Iranians, I did not align myself with any of the Iranian student groups. I graduated from high school and college having limited contact with the Iranian culture.

Consequently, as an Iranian American who migrated to the United States as a child in the early 1970s, I am of neither the iconoclast first generation nor the emerging second generation. I speak Farsi comfortably now and consider myself well informed about Iranian cultural nuances (because I married an Iranian). However, to a first-generation Iranian I am a puzzle. At cultural events, most people in the community consider me, given my age, to be a first generation Iranian or a recent immigrant. Yet my demeanor and ability to participate in social protocol (see chapter two, for example, regarding the tradition of *ta'roffing*) belie my role as an Iranian.

One instance captures how I vacillate in and out of this community. The Iranian Community Center, *Kanoon*, in Newton, Massachusetts, sponsored an event promoted in its newsletter as "an evening with the community." To a researcher in search of participants, this seemed an ideal venue to find Iranians who would know of potential participants. I arrived at this event dressed in jeans, with my two-year-old son who was also dressed very casually. It immediately became evident that I had missed the entire point of the function. An evening with the community implied a space where one would display one's successes through clothing and jewelry. Men were dressed in three-piece suits, the women in glittery long gowns with an abundant display of gems and gold and beauty-salon makeovers. My casual appearance immediately sent shocked looks through the room as though their glares implied "who was this Iranian among us?" The situation was exacerbated by not having my husband accompany me to the gathering. With no husband at my side, the inappropriateness of my behavior seemed to have increased; I seemed to be a single mom who lacked family unity. Consequently, my attire and appearance, presumably acceptable in U.S.-native occasions, were inappropriate to first-generation Iranians in the community center.

This event is just one example of my continual self-interrogation in this study. I place myself both inside and outside of the community that I studied. Royce (1982) would identify me as a "cultural broker" -- someone "who span[s] both the world of the immigrants and the home they have chosen" (p. 135). On the one hand, my Iranian identity allowed me to gain an "insider's perspective" about what my participants were revealing, since I understand most of the subtle dimensions of the Iranian culture. On the other hand, my identity also posed a challenge in that I needed to disconnect my own personal experiences from those of my subjects. Maintaining an open mind to whatever information they revealed was a continual challenge (Miles & Huberman, 1994). This dual position of being both an insider and an outsider, according to Westkott (1990), "is not only a source of knowledge and insight, but also a source of self-criticism" (p. 59). I was able to use a dual perspective to analyze my data.

Entry

Many qualitative researchers have offered strategies for dealing with problems of entry (Beck, 1970; Dalton, 1959; Marshall, 1984; Rossman, 1984; Wax, 1971). As I have already mentioned, Iranians are distrustful of researchers. The most important factor that helped me gain access to this community was my affiliation with Harvard, rather than my role as an Iranian American. However, as I elaborate further below, my affiliation with Harvard may have also affected the way in which students composed their responses.

Ethics

From the outset of this study, I knew that the life histories and experiences of my participants were connected to other Iranians in this country and even some still living in Iran. Though the interview is essentially a social interaction that involves of a relationship between the interviewer and the informant, Gilligan (1982) and Kohlberg (1971) have discussed how the researcher-subject dyad extends beyond the two to encompass other lives. In this way, the information my participants shared not only revealed characteristics of the participants themselves, but also of others in their circle of family and friends.

One way I chose to address the issue of trust and ethics in my study was to provide each participant with my own personal history in this country and how my experiences, like theirs, have not been represented in the literature concerning immigrants and their education. Since the entire interviewer-participant relationship rests on a pivotal time period (as in the case of my interviews), it was important to me to have subjects feel that the sharing was reciprocal and that a "conversation with a purpose" was developing (Kahn & Cannell, 1957, p.149). I was careful, however, not to lead the participants toward particular issues.

As a second approach to developing trust, I sent the participants transcripts of the interviews and encouraged them to edit, modify, and/or delete any comments that they did not feel comfortable with my using in the analysis. In many ways, this extended the dialogue beyond our interview since I was able to ask them to clarify the comments they had made during the interview. None of the students returned the transcripts with edits; however, two of them needed to be reassured that their names would not be included. Finally, I ensured as much anonymity as I possibly could. I promised that neither their names nor the names of the institutions with which they were affiliated would be mentioned in my study together.

Site Selection

On the one hand, as home to many colleges and universities, Massachusetts is ideal for a study involving undergraduate students. The diversity of campuses allowed me to cast a wide net in terms of participants' backgrounds. The area also attracts students from far away, allowing me to interview students who grew up in California, Washington, D.C., Texas, and New York. Moreover, the convenience of proximity, in terms of scheduling interviews with sporadic student schedules, also made it ideal.

On the other hand, unlike California, New York, and Washington, D.C., Massachusetts does not have a large permanent Iranian community. This made it particularly difficult to identify participants within designated subgroups, such as those within the Iranian Jewish community. This latter point forced me to go outside Massachusetts and interview a number of Iranian Jews who lived and studied around New York City.

The Participants

I used a variety of approaches to identify participants. I contacted the Persian Clubs at four schools: Brandeis, Tufts, MIT, and Harvard. (Note that only one participant actually belonged to and/or participated in the activities of one of these clubs.) The problem with identifying students directly via these clubs was that they were either graduate students and therefore did not fit the profile of my study and/or they did not have active meetings where students would gather. Rather, the Persian clubs provided me access to students who would know of students in their respective schools who fit the profile of my study. Five of my participants came from such referrals. This approach had an additional advantage: I did not necessarily find second-generation Iranians who were, by the nature of their involvement in a cultural club, biased about their responses. That is, their self-selection as members of these clubs may have indicated an existing bias toward their culture.

Throughout the interviewing process, I discovered that many of my participants had taken a course relating to Iran – history, political science, Farsi language, Middle Eastern religions, etc. I sought out professors at various schools and asked them to identify any students who had taken a course with them. Both an advantage and a disadvantage to this approach was that students who typically chose such courses had an interest in the Iranian culture. I found only one participant through this approach. I also found participants by asking Iranian professors about their students in noncultural courses.

To find Armenian Iranians, I distributed flyers at an Armenian church in Watertown whose membership was mostly comprised of Iranians; local sundry and carpet stores; the Iranian-Armenian Association of Boston; the Iranian-American Cultural Center; and the Hairenick Association (Armenian newspaper).

The most difficult part of my search for participants was finding Iranian Jews. In the New England area, I could not find any organization or location where they congregated. Fortuitously, I made contact with a respected individual within the Mashadi Jewish community of New York. I used his wide network of friends and acquaintances to find participants – both Mashadi and non-Mashadi Jews -- through the snowball process. Two of the four males and two of the five Jewish Iranian participants where from this Mashadi community.

My search for Bahá'ís was perhaps the most interesting. After several months of fruitless searching for Bahá'í participants, I decided to "drop" this component of my study. So many confidentiality issues surrounded this highly persecuted community that I did not want to push the limits of potential participants' trust. Then, by chance, two Bahá'ís found out about my study through the flyers I had distributed and through the other members of the study who had passed on word that I was looking for such individuals. The connection to these two participants led me to find two other Bahá'ís who also elected to participate in this study.

Sample Characteristics

The findings of this study are based on open-ended, in-depth interviews with thirty Iranian-American college students, between eighteen and twenty-eight years of age. Thirteen of them identified themselves as Muslims, nine as Jewish, four as Bahá'ís, and four as Armenians. At this point, I would like to expand upon two issues that emerged through this self-identification.

The participants who identified themselves as Muslim repeatedly mentioned the problems they had with identifying themselves with this category. One male Muslim participant summed it up by saying, "religion for Iroonis in the second generation is pretty much nonexistent." And, another female Muslim participant said that other than her family not eating pork, she did not consider herself to be Muslim. One can argue that the notion of religion being absent from their daily lives is typical of many modern adolescents, regardless of nationality and/or religion. However, these college students struggled with having the term "Muslim" used to describe them. They told me that the term is wrought with negative stereotypes in American society: "Muslims are seen as

terrorists." Even my Armenian participants commented on
their frustrations at being identified as Muslim because they
said, Americans typically associate anyone from Iran as
being Muslim. They were keen on making it clear to those
around them that they were not Muslim. A female
Armenian said for example, "Muslims are looked down
upon, so I stress I am Christian but I am from Iran, I'm
Armenian; I differentiate between the two." In light of
these points, I debated how to identify the participants I had
categorized as Muslim, for in many ways it is a misleading
portrayal of my participants. As a researcher with feet in
both cultural contexts, I understood their reservations. The
extent to which participants practiced and lived within the
Muslim faith varied dramatically. While I continued to
categorize the respondents under such a header, I
underscore this point throughout the remaining sections.

The largest number of participants were Muslim
women. I originally interviewed a number of Muslim
women and as a result of these preliminary interviews, I
was prompted to modify the interview protocol.
Consequently, I interviewed additional female Muslims to
ensure that I had addressed my new inquiries. Table 7
below presents the breakdown between male and female
participants.

Table 7: Sample Breakdown

Ethno-religiosity	Male	Female
Muslim	4	9
Jewish	4	5
Bahá'í	2	2
Armenian	2	2
TOTAL	12	18

My original aim was to interview eight Muslims, eight
Jews, and eight Armenians. But as Lincoln and Guba
(1985) state, research can "unfold, cascade, roll, and
emerge" (p. 210); this was the case with my sample. My
preliminary attempt to find Bahá'ís was fruitless, so I
proposed that I drop Bahá'ís from my study and instead

include only the major ethnic-religious groups: Muslims, Jews, and Armenians. Yet, as described earlier, once I was in the process of finding participants and distributing flyers and contacting various members in the Iranian community, four Bahá'ís willingly came forward to participate. Ironically, the group that I felt had least to fear in terms of persecution back in Iran, Armenians, turned out to be the most difficult to recruit for the study. And, as I will discuss in my findings, the invisibility of Armenians' Iranian identity affects their desire to be identified and/or to be included in research pertaining to Iranians.

I had two other criteria for choosing participants: they had to be enrolled in an undergraduate college program, and both of their parents had to have been born in Iran. Children of bicultural marriages would have had a different experience growing up in the United States, the exploration of which was beyond the limits of my study.

The majority of students in this sample varied between eighteen and twenty-eight years of age. Their average age was twenty-one; two students were quite above this average, one being an Armenian student who had elected to take some time off after high school to raise money for her education, the other a Bahá'í student whose family had faced similar financial restrictions. Most participants, then, were either born in Iran and/or had migrated to the United States prior to their elementary education; only five students had attended elementary school in Iran before their family's migration (three came at the age of seven, one at nine, and one at twelve).

The time of family migration for 80 percent of my sample was after the Revolution. A closer look at family migration shows that the largest number of participants' families had migrated to the United States during 1979 – the year of the Iranian Revolution; and nearly all were Jewish. A handful of families had migrated here prior to the revolution – three Muslim, one Jewish, and two Bahá'í families. Their pre-Revolutionary family migration status correlates to several other factors, such as having U.S.-

educated parents and a better sense of the American educational system.

The educational and occupational differences between fathers and mothers of these second-generation Iranian students is striking.[45] Perhaps this is a byproduct of the gender-defined occupational roles of the culture from which they came. Fathers of these students had noticeably greater levels of education and higher status occupations, while the mothers, despite respectable levels of education, held traditional low-status occupations: teaching, seamstress, homemakers. Many mothers assisted their husbands in the family business, such as a floral shop or a dental office. Most participants said that while they were growing up their mothers had stayed at home and only when the kids had grown up had they elected to go to work. Interestingly, two women who at the time of this study were researchers at prominent American universities were part of the student cohort who came to study in the U.S. under the Shah and who had then gone back to Iran. They had returned to the United States after the Revolution and were more successful at integrating themselves into the American work force than those Iranians who migrated for the first time after the Revolution.

The fathers' education levels are relatively high as compared to native-born Americans as well as other immigrant groups (see chapter two). Among the group itself, they are highest among the Muslim group; seven of the thirteen had either a medical or a doctoral degree; five had a masters degree; and only one had a bachelors degree. Three of the nine Jewish fathers had medical and doctoral degrees, the remaining six a bachelors degree. Interestingly, among this group the majority were self-employed – either in their own practice or business. Among the Bahá'ís and the Armenians, the highest level of education was a bachelors degree; only one Bahá'í father had his medical degree, and he had migrated here in 1976. The lower level of education among Bahá'ís and Armenians reflects two issues. One, for Bahá'ís, access to education was limited in Iran. Two, for Armenians, who traditionally held merchant professions in Iran, extended formal schooling was not as relevant.

Perhaps more interesting is the schooling of the students themselves. Four of the thirty students had attended private schools (elementary and high school), two of which were religious schools (one Armenian; one Jewish).[46] In general, most attended public schools. However, I should note that the overwhelming majority of these public schools were located in affluent White suburban neighborhoods where the quality of education often matches that of private schools. Regardless of socioeconomic status, I found that it was an educational tactic that the parents used to get their children a quality education. Even those who could not afford to buy a house in an affluent community rented their residence so that their children could attend its public school.

The colleges and universities these students attended included public and private. The number-one criteria for choosing a particular institution of higher education had to do with its proximity to the family residence. Nearly all the students in this sample (with the exception of two female Muslims who were originally from the West Coast) said that their main reason for choosing the college or university they had was so that they could be close to their family. The farthest they were willing to be away was a two-hour drive. Their college majors were limited to fields that were based on math or science (business, pre-med, pre-law). Only one student fell out of the norm with a communications major.

Interviews

I obtained multiple perspectives on the educational experiences of second-generation Iranian students. I initially conducted at least two individual interviews based on a semi-structured interview protocol. In the first interview, my approach was intentionally a nondirective, conversational approach in an attempt to encourage the students to discuss what they deemed important. I gathered data that included background information and educational history, as well as information about their present experiences and the links they see between past events and their current educational attainment. In subsequent interviews I asked more focused questions. These questions uncovered information about the students' educational histories, how families used their resources for educating their children, the nature of their family lives, the nature of their relationships with the larger Iranian community, and their reasons for pursuing higher education.

Yet, following a two-interview approach was extremely problematic in that I was losing many participants. Scheduling the second interview, I found, was often more difficult than scheduling the first. I, therefore, weighed the benefits and disadvantages of my two-interview approach and decided it was more important not to lose participants in the course of the study. Hence, I changed to a one (often two-hour) interview method.

The interview protocol evolved throughout the interview process. For example, one topic repeatedly came up throughout the interviews – the role of the dinner table in their household. The dinner table was repeatedly analogized as the locus of the development of their cultural identity. This was where the family gathered, and students often used this topic to distinguish themselves from their American peers. Having overlooked the importance of this facet of their lives in my earliest interviews, I pursued this theme/question throughout the remaining interviews. Another example of the evolution of the interview protocol regards the question of whether the participants could speak (read/write) Farsi. I realized that this was a misleading question for Armenians, who grew up with Armenian as their first language and Farsi as their second. I thus modified my question to, "What language do you typically use at home?" The repetition of themes that I had not anticipated when constructing the interview protocol led me to add questions to my original interview guide. For example, I had completely neglected to inquire about dating – something that was at the core of their college social life. Though I added some questions, I deleted others that continuously came up as irrelevant in the interviews. For example, I asked students whether they had experienced any obstacles in their educational experiences. Repeatedly, the answers were "no" or "not really," and they expressed that this question was not really relevant in their experiences.

I conducted all interviews in English. None of my participants made any attempt to converse with me in Farsi, though in numerous interviews the participants made some use of the Farsi language – whether describing something that had no equivalent in English and/or to identify with me on an Iranian level. The interjection of Farsi in the interviews illuminates my role as a "cultural insider" and how the meaning derived from the interview would have been different had I not spoken a common language with my participants.

All interviews were recorded and transcribed. I used pseudonyms for all names mentioned in the interview, including those of the participants, the institutions to which they referred, and/or their relatives in the U.S. or in Iran. I sent either an electronic or a hard copy of the transcripts to the participants asking them to delete, modify, or add any comments that made them more at ease with what they had revealed.

Interviews took place in locations deemed most convenient by participants. The typical setting for the interviews was their school library, though I also held interviews in students' dormitory rooms and homes, as well as in my office at Harvard.

After each interview I composed an analytic memo that included information about the interview process. I noted my initial impressions of our interview. For example, one female participant had asked me to meet her in her dormitory. When I arrived there she had a small traditional table set up for a guest, with fruit, nuts, and pastry – a symbol of "Iranian hospitality." In another interview, one male participant revealed his frustration with the Iranian community only after I had turned the recorder off; I recorded this in a post-interview analytic memo. In yet another interview, I found it noteworthy that my participant cried while sharing the hardship her parents had endured in Texas during the hostage crisis, and I was moved by another participant's insights as to how his father's abuse – mental and physical – had left an impact on his family's life. I recorded the subtle expressions and moments that were not captured on tape in these post-interview memos.

Transcribing the Interviews

Transcription of interviews paralleled data collection. This enabled me to reflect on my interviewing technique and refine the questions I was asking. At this time, I also composed a second analytic memo. In this memo I sketched the patterns that I thought were beginning to emerge.

I chose to transcribe the interviews myself for two reasons. First, I wanted to be able to listen to the interview again and create a preliminary list of emerging themes. Second, I did not want a third party to jeopardize my promise of privacy to the participants.

Copies of transcripts were mailed to participants if they had so requested using regular or electronic mail. I sent a note with the transcripts, reiterating that I would be using pseudonyms to refer to them and their academic institutions.

Data Analysis

I used two analytic strategies to examine the educational experiences of second- generation Iranian undergraduate college students: case study narratives (Patton, 1990) and case-ordered descriptive meta-matrices (Miles & Huberman, 1994).

Case Study Narratives

Since my research question explored the experiences of individuals, I created each individual's story as a systematic case record. Each of the thirty case records contextualizes the student narratives. The case study approach, particularly appropriate for answering "how" questions, helped me generate themes (Marshall & Rossman, 1995). Case study narratives, for example, include but are not limited to describing students' family background, the circumstances of their family's migration, their experiences in the American education system, their ambitions, and the extent to which they align themselves with Iranian culture. I, therefore, present the events, factors, and experiences imparted by my participants that have led to their academic attainment.

Case-Ordered Descriptive Meta-Matrices

As a second step in the data analysis process, I created a series of case-ordered descriptive meta-matrices (Miles & Huberman, 1994). Using descriptive data from the case narratives I generated "internally consistent or contradictory" themes across the thirty participants (Anderson & Jack, 1991).

Five consistent themes emerged from the data: family, culture, socioeconomic status, peers, and schools. Yet these themes contradicted one another on several dimensions: religious-ethnicity, whether their family migrated before or after the Revolution (wave), whether they were born in the U.S. or migrated at an early age (1.5/2.0), gender, and whether they grew up on the East or West Coast. The following table outlines the variability of the themes along these dimensions.

The matrix analysis led me to discover the relationship between themes, such as how family and culture overlapped: each student's culture was really based on that of their family.

Table 8: Meta-Matrix of the Relationship Between Themes and Dimensions.

	Family	Culture	SES	Peers	Schools
Religious-ethnicity					
Wave					
1.5/2.0					
Gender					
East/West					

There were also relationships between dimensions, for instance, the culture that the students embraced was really predicated on their family's socioeconomic status. I thus created two additional matrices examining the relationship between each of my themes and dimensions. In this second matrix, I summarize the relationship between the themes, and in the next chapter I discuss how these themes overlapped.

Table 9: Analysis of the relationship between themes

	Family	Culture	SES	Peers	Schools
Family	*				
Culture		*			
SES			*		
Peers				*	
Schools					*

There were also relationships between each of the dimensions (religious-ethnicity, wave, 1.5/2.0, gender, and whether they came from the East or the West Coast). For example, religious-ethnicity and the time when a family migrated to the United States were often highly related; most Jewish Iranians migrated before or at the height of the Iranian Revolution. Or, the role of gender as it related to dating, for example, depended on religious background. Table 10 summarizes the relationship between these dimensions.

My findings, then, were arranged in four ways. First, I examined each individual's case record. Second, I looked into how each theme varied across each dimension.

Table 10: Analysis of the Relationship between Dimensions

	Religious -ethnicity	Wave	1.5/2.0	Gender	East/West
Religious-ethnicity	*				
Wave		*			
1.5/2.0			*		
Gender				*	
East/West					*

Third, I considered what the relationships were among various themes. And, finally, I investigated whether the relationship between each dimension played a role in my findings.

A Methodological Consideration

The data collected, analyzed and reported in this dissertation is representative of a singular point in time. I am aware that I have not captured the entire span of these students' lives and that I have only scratched the surface of the landscape of their experiences as children of Iranian immigrants. As Maxwell (1992) states:

> Interviewing poses some special problems for internal generalizability because the researcher usually is in the presence of the person interviewed only briefly, and must necessarily draw inferences from what happened during that brief period to the rest of the informant's life, including his or her actions and perspectives. An account based on interviews may be descriptively, interpretively, and theoretically valid as an account of the person's

actions and perspective in that interview, but may miss other aspects of the person's perspectives that were not expressed in the interview, and can easily lead to false inferences about his or her actions outside the interview situation. (p. 294)

This methodological approach enabled me to gain insight into the lives of second-generation Iranians that I hope to will open future lines of inquiry.

CHAPTER FOUR

Education: An Unparallel Path

[I]t was never an issue if I would go to college. Education is what gave my family everything it has today. My dad came to this country with five things: he came to this country with a wife, a daughter, a suitcase, $130 in his pocket, and an education. And the education: that helped him out and that was it, the most important thing. If it wasn't for that education he wouldn't have the life that we do.

[M]oney is materialistic and it can be taken away from you, but education, you earn it and nobody can take that away from you -- the one thing that you have that nobody can take away from you, or you know, separate you from that.

The participants in this study have all been brought up with a strong need to pursue education. Where and how was this need nurtured? Flippantly, though insightfully, many participants remarked that they were "inoculated at birth" as to the importance of their college education. Regardless of socioeconomic, ethnic or religious background, second-

generation Iranians in this study highly prized education --
a path with no parallel. As the above quotes illustrate,
education offered them social status and financial success.
So strong was this value of education that none of the
participants ever considered a path other than college. A
female Muslim participant, puzzled by the irrelevance of
such questions, thought it implausible to think of any other
choices after high school. "But what would I do with
myself instead? Like it just didn't seem, what was the
alternative if I didn't go to college?" said one female
Muslim participant.

An interesting aspect of my interviews was that all
participants, with only one exception, had picked a major
based on either math or science. Perhaps a by-product of
the Iranian system of education that exalted the math and
science, or perhaps a reflection of their fathers' career paths
(nearly all fathers were in math and sciences themselves)
these students seemed to hold similar convictions about
these fields as evinced in the Iranian society. When I asked
why they had gravitated towards math and science, they
expressed their beliefs that these majors were of the
greatest relative utility:

Education is more of a luxury than it is a necessity
for [Americans] here. I look at their [Americans]
majors for example, we have more I would say hard
core majors like science, psychology, as opposed to
art history or uhm I don't know music. The majors
tend to be a bit more ... I think .... tougher majors.
It's not like Americans who take "heart-driven"
majors, they like something and just major in it as
opposed to us who have to take advantage [of
education] more. You see, we take tougher majors
even if we don't really like it that much but we see
more of a future in it ... than for example, I don't
know, an easier major because its something you
like.

The one student who had picked a liberal arts major was aware that her choice did not fit in the Iranian educational model:

> If you don't go to college you are not up to standards, up to Iranian standards. Uhm and if you go into college and you don't go into a medical school or a law school and you go into something like the liberal arts they feel, that's what I think, that you are not smart enough for you don't have enough … you're not … college material, I guess.

What factors lay behind their educational attitude? The single most common adjective that second-generation Iranian students used to describe themselves academically was "self-motivated." Whether they attended Harvard or Boston University, and whether they were Jewish, Muslim, Bahá'í or Armenian, they repeatedly used "self-motivation" as the reason behind their educational attainment. I refer to it here as their zeal for education. When asked to elaborate on their definition of "self-motivation," or this educational zeal, they described a complex braid of family and culture.

Family & Culture: What Was Relevant

The two most salient factors in the educational outlook of this sample were family and culture. The boundaries between them are sometimes unclear: one can hardly speak of one without considering the other. Yet, to understand the nature of each in the lives of these students one needs to first present them in separate spheres and then bring them together as I do later in this section.

Family

When I look back I think of how they came here with nothing and they tried to get the American dream, you know they tried to struggle and they bought the house and they bought the car, they live better now than most of my friends who are American. Actually this is ironic because being from Texas my friends' parents are concerned with themselves, not so much in their children, their future, they don't really put so much emphasis and ambitions in their children as much as they do worrying about their own retirement and their personal health. And that is completely different from my mom and dad. They actually work so hard just to make sure that my sister and I can have the education that they couldn't have.

Family has played an immense role in the construction of the educational outlooks of participants in this study and was cited unanimously by all as the only reason for their academic maturation. What features characterize the family environment that so propelled these students to value education? There was a wide range of differences among these students – some families had migrated to the United States before the revolution and some after; some families were influenced by the traditions of their religious faith more than others; and still others had financial wealth whereas some of the other families did not. Still, it is possible to isolate a distinct family context within this tremendous diversity.

Point of Reference

Despite wide variances among the families of these second-generation Iranian students, one point resonated throughout all their lives. They understood that they had far more educational opportunities than their parents and it was up to them to take advantage of what they have been offered. In essence, their families had given them a point of reference. Some families made this point explicitly to their children, while others made the message implicit through conversations overheard on the telephone with friends and relatives, or by the very fact that they escaped Iran. Education was something that had either given the parents of participants everything they had in this country, or it was something that was denied them in Iran which they were determined to make available to their children. It was the comparison between the past and the present (parents' generation and the students) and between the United States and Iran today that forged a powerful belief in the value of education. The following two female Jewish-Iranians realized the opportunities they were afforded that their parents had not:

My parents had experiences and I always have those experiences in mind, and think how lucky I am. No matter how stressed I get from school, I think I never had to go through what my family had to go through. That makes being in America -- for me to go to school, to be the year book editor, to play the violin, to go to Jewish day school, to being on my own – 'you have it pretty good.'

I mean it's self-motivation but it's also the fact that you are coming from another country to like America – land of opportunity. Like my mom told me this the other day actually, that my aunts who just moved to Israel from Iran a little while ago that we're like what makes them proud. Because we're in America and me and my sister are getting an education, and we are going to be something. We're looked at as very lucky to be here in terms of my family overseas. And that works as self-motivation for me, so like achievement and success has always been important to me.

His family's persecution in Iran worked as a powerful point of reference for this male Bahá'í:

Just knowing, just seeing my mom and dad crying when we got a phone call about someone who got murdered, like a cousin who got murdered in Iran. Knowing that my grandmother can never leave the country, and knowing that I can never go into the

country. And not understanding why. Not seeing
any of my family for over twenty years. Knowing
people who have tried to escape and have been
killed, knowing my uncles were innocent and have
spent like 17 years in prison, being pulled over for
no reason and being beaten, going to prison and
losing their identity. So many of my uncles have
gone to prison for no reason.

As her point of reference, this female Bahá'í cited the fact
that the Bahá'ís were not allowed to obtain an education in
Iran:

As you know it's difficult for any one to go to the
university in Iran. So for Bahá'ís there is no chance.
The highest education you can get in Iran as a
Bahá'í is a high school education. Especially in the
Bahá'í community education is highly spoken of,
it's very encouraged, even for females it's highly
encouraged.

A female Muslim participant, in the following example,
mentions how the Iranian Revolution generally continues to
resonate in her family's life. It is an example of how a
cataclysmic family experience continues to create point of
reference for their lives in America. It also exemplifies the
existence of wanting to preserve one's culture in this
country while concurrently taking advantage of its
structural (academic and economic) opportunities. It is the
opposition of two forms of assimilation: cultural versus
structural.

My parents came from a country that had a
revolution. When you experience a revolution and
the dramatic changes it causes in your society, and
in your life, you develop this kind of need to keep
close to your people while at the same time wanting
to go out to make a difference; to be successful.

She continues to explain that although her parents have transplanted their lives to America, their tie to Iran continues to be strong; a bond her parents transmit to their children:

My dad makes donations to Iran versus here 'cause he's like "I am going to help my soil, my blood" and he always says "you will never lose love and respect for your country. I can never lose the love I have for Iran because it's my blood, I want to be buried in Iran." That's how I feel Iran.

For a female Muslim student, and for a female Bahá'í student, knowing of opportunities they have here that their cousins back in Iran did not have formed their point of reference:

We're the only ones here in America. And, I feel like it's my duty, I'm here, I have the opportunity, I can achieve so much here, I mean I don't have any exams like the *concour* [national college entrance examinations] blocking me, there are no obstacles. I can achieve anything and that's why I feel I should. Being here I should take advantage of it and get the education, get the opportunity.

I would feel guilty if I slacked in any way. Knowing that so many Bahá'í brothers and sisters in Iran who don't have the opportunity in Iran. I would feel guilty to have so much at my hands and not to take advantage of it. Like my mother told me that sometimes she feels guilty for leaving Iran and not putting up with things like other Bahá'ís have. She feels she took the easy way out. But then she tells me that she doesn't feel guilty unless she gets caught up in the materialistic western world. As long as she is using the opportunities here to benefit humanity -- instead of escaping just to have an easy

life in America -- then she doesn't feel guilty. So I
think that's one of the reasons we have that drive.
We were told to take advantage of it and not just
throw it away.

In the following example, it was an explicit message from
her parents that served as this young woman's point of
reference:

> I think that was one of my parents' influences on
> me, like we brought you to America, we brought
> you and your brother to the states so that you could
> succeed. If we didn't want you to have so many
> different opportunities then we would just stayed.
> There was a war we could have all been killed you
> know but we sacrificed everything for you .... I was
> kind of in this environment that there wasn't, you
> didn't have a choice. So this is it: you came here
> because your parents sacrificed for you and you
> better succeed.

With families as a key factor in the lives of these students,
references to Iran became engrained as a motivating factor
behind their education. Their families created a point of
reference from which they compared the educational
opportunities they have in this country.

Autonomy & Respect

While the value of education was instilled in these students,
students noted that their parents were involved in their
schooling. That is, there was a family expectation that
education was important but when it came to their
schooling, parents expected their children to make their
own decisions. Moreover, none of the students described
feeling pressured by their parents to do well in school.
They rarely asked if they had done their homework,
infrequently visited teachers and/or their schools, and did
not help with college choice decisions. Educational

decisions were left to the discretion of the students themselves. One participant remarked that treating his education as his own "business" gave him the autonomy to do well:

> In high school they never asked me what grades I had, they never asked me what I was doing, if they asked me to do my homework I was particularly impressed, (laugh) cuz I figured as long as I do well in school it's my own business. It was sort of a boundary drawn I felt that it was something of my own, it was like my own business.

Parental involvement was extremely limited for all these students, in some instances because of unfamiliarity with the educational system.[47] Parents did not push their children to get only A's or to be honor students. Instead, the underlying theme was that if they were doing their best, their parents were pleased. That is, none of the parents put guilt on their children, saying that they had made sacrifices so they could do well in school. The students felt that when it came to their education, their parents had given them autonomy. Feeling that they had autonomy in making their own educational choices allowed them to feel that their parents respected their decision-making which in turn produced respect for their parents.

> I picked the schools that I wanted to go to, they didn't want me to do anything, obviously they wanted the best for their child but they didn't say you have to go to Harvard or you have to go you know. They just wanted the best for me and they thought I was responsible enough to make that decision.

> I think they were involved in that they weren't involved in a way. That they just left it up to me and

they just said that if you do well in school it's for
your own good.

I guess you could say that their involvement with
my education up to college was pretty minimal.
They constantly were stressing the value of an
education but I don't see that as being you know, a
great deal of involvement. It may have served as
some sort of a motivation but it wasn't any
involvement. Actually, they weren't even really
pushing me in terms of my grades, they didn't even
really question me in that sense either.

Despite the espoused "laissez faire" attitude towards the
details and daily events of children's education, parents and
families influenced educational decisions in other ways.
The number one criterion cited by nearly all of the
participants as their reason for choosing a
college/university was to be close to family. This sentiment
was strongest among female Iranian Jews and a rule for
Mashadi female Jews, who were mandated by their parents
to stay local.[48] But others, even Armenian males, cited
distance to family as their primary criterion for choosing
their college/university. Those who had ventured farthest
were two Muslim females -- one from California, and the
other from Texas. Yet, ironically, these two Iranian-Muslim
females both felt that they had gained much status with
their family for choosing New England, a serious academic
environment, for their studies. So, in some respects, it was
their families who had propelled them to head East as a
means of gaining respect.
     The triangulated combination of point of reference,
educational autonomy, and respect created a sense of
purpose and a dedication to education for these students. In
the next section, I will explain the variations due to family
background and family structure.

Variable Family Structures

Family structure varied from student to student. For some, "family" consisted of one parent: their mother (two were widows, and three others' husbands had abandoned their families after migrating to this country). For some of the others, the family unit was solely comprised of the nuclear family, with little or no contact with any other family members in Iran or the United States. For the Jewish Iranians who grew up in Great Neck, New York, family extended to the community. For many of the participants, "family" also included Iranian family friends who had taken on the role of extended family in the United States, something I refer to here as pseudo-families. These included other nearby Iranian families who would get together regularly. "When I was growing up almost all the Iranian families I knew were extended families," said one male Iranian Muslim participant who grew up in Rhode Island. His interaction with these fellow expatriates was similar to most of the other participants who often even referred to these family friends as "*khaleh*" (aunt) or "*amoo*" (uncle), exemplifying that the nature of their relationship to their family was similar to that of extended family.

The family boundary, then, was sometimes drawn at the immediate family (parents and siblings) and/or beyond to include a broader group. And it was within this family structure that the point of reference, educational autonomy, and respect were nurtured.

Significance of Family Life

> I think the most important thing is the family. 'Cause over here it's not like that. The friends I've had in high school they didn't care about their family. The most important people were their friends. And they'd sacrifice everything for their

friends, which is kind of nice but at the same time I don't think you should just let go of your family.

To nurture anything within any family structure, people must first put value on family. If family did not take the primary place in the lives of these students, then the families' point of reference, autonomy, and respect that they gave would not work in the influential ways that it did. Where family was an integral part, it had a lot of bearing on the students' decisions. Ostensibly, if they felt less connected to family, they would have been less influenced. For example, had family not been important to these students, then their parents' references to the "old" country would have been construed as negative; autonomy would pave the way for breaking off from the family.

Because a strong belief and emphasis on the importance of family were present, the three factors of point of reference, autonomy, and respect coalesced in various family structures and with various family backgrounds to have a positive impact on their educational experiences. Many of these students considered their family, particularly their parents, as contributing to their academic outlook:

> I guess it would be my parents, yeah, definitely, my parents are my support, and the way they raised us -- they were so involved in our life. It wasn't like 'oh they're my parents [negative]' – I'd tell them everything! And they'd knew everything about my life and they were very involved very concerned about everything….Like my parents never yell at me if I don't do well in school you know they're just like, "as long as you tried your hardest…" you know, that is very self-motivating.

The family's position of importance described by these students represented an archetypal difference between themselves and their American counterparts. Many said that their American friends had limited respect for their parents; many heard their friends use profane language towards or in front of their parents. Conversely, they said that the parents of their friends thought more of their own welfare than of their children's. One male Muslim explains:

In America parents kick their kids out when they're 18. Most of my friends don't go home, they live in college all year round. Their parents go off do things, like cruises, vacations, they do whatever. We all get together. We just spent three weeks in the house [for our vacation]. The main thing is that we are all together.

A note regarding their family values is that all of the students described those in their families, and usually one parent in particular, as role models. For some, it was their mothers. For others, the role model was outside the immediate family; and for one female Armenian participant her father-in-law took on that role. One male Jewish participant's response captures the connection between family and role models. "I try to take a piece of everyone in my family."

It would be misleading to conclude that family dynamics alone created their academic drive. One could argue that any "good" parent would value education and give their children freedom to maneuver him or herself within that framework. Instead, my participants drew the distinction that it was the interplay between this fairly typical parenting characteristic and unique cultural characteristics that paved the course of their academic outlook.

Culture: Iranian "Hyphen" American[49]

Coupled with family, culture was the second leading factor in the educational outlook of these students. To say that culture played a role in the academic lives of these students is problematic in many ways. After all, how one defines culture, Iranian and/or American is highly complex (see next chapter). And, the hyphen in their national identity would suggest, culture was a factor that bridged two landscapes, making the notion of culture ever more convoluted.

Left of the Hyphen: Iranian

> It's very easy to lose who you are here in America. I mean you can't forget your background but to lose that connection with being an Iranian is very easy to do here. And not just being an Iranian, any immigrants or foreigners here is very easy to lose that. For example I see it with the Asians. There are a lot of Asians here and I see them like in my high school, this girl would say to me, "I hate my family, they're so strict and they still think they're you know they still live in China or whatever they don't realize we're in America and things are different and they should treat us differently you know." The impression I get from them is that you should just let go of it ... and just accept the culture that's here.

On one side, their sense of having an Iranian background was powerful among these participants. Nurtured in the home/family environment, their sense of being an "Iranian" was part and parcel of the point of reference. These students felt that they possessed something that their fellow "American" students did not possess. For some, it was their ability to speak Farsi, for others the roots of their ancestry. Still for others, their home environment – where walls are adorned with Iranian artifacts, Iranian food is served, and Iranian music played – serves as a reminder of their connection to another culture. The specific nature of Iranian culture is, however, a multifaceted concept, defined differently by each of the four religious-ethnic groups and assumed a different shape and form from family to family. For those who apprehensively called themselves Muslim, the celebration of the Persian New Year, Noruz, was central to their definition of the Iranian culture, yet vague and distant to their co-nationals who were either Armenian, Jewish, or Bahá'í.[50] Culture for these second-generation Iranians can be best defined as bits and pieces of what their parents brought with them to the United States upon migration – in their suitcases, in their memories, in their stories.

One male Bahá'í student captured the essence of what his parents brought over:

> The greatest thing my parents took away from Iran was their religion. So if you talk about what they brought from Iran, it would definitely be the Bahá'í faith. I think it's the greatest thing that they've taken away.... and given to their children.

For each family the prominent components of the Iranian culture differed, depending on their religious-ethnic backgrounds. Yet despite the spectrum of definitions surrounding the Iranian culture among the four religious-ethnic groups, the "dinner table" topic was common to all definitions. Repeatedly, the dinner table was used as an example of where they ate "their mother's Iranian cooking," where they "heard their parents speak Farsi (or Armenian)," or sometimes heard references to Iran. In essence, the dinner table became the unifying symbol across all their varying descriptions of the Iranian culture.

I should note, however, that since most had never experienced life in Iran themselves they had no (or limited) exposure to the Iranian culture. They admitted their confusion as to what constitutes the Iranian culture: the culture derived from their faith, and/or the culture espoused by their family – both overlapping but not necessarily the same as the Iranian culture.

> I don't even know the difference, I don't even know the value system is different because we are Jewish or because we are Persian. So I don't know why she tells me to do certain things. Or not do certain

things. I don't know if Muslim Persians have the same stand on this so I wouldn't know.

In many respects, the way that they had acquired the Iranian culture was implicit — through their parents' conversation with each other and with friends. In the following quotes, my participants explain that the Iranian culture has been transferred to them through informal mechanisms:

> In daily conversation. A lot of it in hearing [my parents] talk to other people -- telephone, or when they have their friends over. You just get the idea of what it's about.

> I've heard them at like these huge Iranian gatherings and with people their age and they'll talk about issues and some people will have tears in their eyes and they will get emotional and listen to really classic Persian music talk about issues in Iran.

By absorbing the culture indirectly, nearly all the participants commented on how precarious their understanding of the Iranian culture was. For example, this male Bahá'í student told me:

> For any kid like me [second generation Iranians] what we think of the Iranian culture is very warped, 'cause we don't really have a grasp of what it really is. Iranian culture for me is defined by the things that are miniscule, defined by language, defined by gestures of people, defined by the food, defined by what I know of the politics, and the history of the country. But the real feeling of the country is not there, obviously, because I've never been there, so I don't know really.

The uncertainty of their Iranian culture became manifest when second-generation Iranians were brought together, often on a college campus. As a by-product of the geographical dispersion of Iranians in the United States, most of those who I interviewed had grown up without knowing other Iranians their age during high school to create a basis for understanding their culture. (The exceptions were those who grew up in Great Neck, New York, California and Texas where there are large concentration of Iranians). As they were growing up, typically, interaction with other Iranians their age was limited to family gatherings or Farsi classes. Upon arrival at college they came into contact with other Iranians.

> I think it's really problematic to think that your only access to Iranian culture has been just one family group or maybe close friends. What happens if those things aren't representative of what it means to be an Iranian? Then the culture you define, the way you define yourself, isn't correct. So when you meet other people who define themselves as Iranian you are going to have problems, you will say something and others won't understand it.

Through vague methods, they would decide who amongst them can be established as knowledgeable about being an "Iranian." Deciphering who among them was the "Iranian cultural connoisseur," then, was based on two over-riding criteria: who had the most command of Farsi, and/or whether they were born in Iran or the United States (1.5 generation versus 2nd-generation). In the following quote, this male participant explains how he and his peers determine their cultural hierarchy:

> There are three or four Iranians that hung out together and there was always this guy last year who'd be with them and I was introduced to him a couple of times and he was always introduced to me

as Eddie. And none of the guys told me he was Persian, this year I found out that he's Iranian. He spoke in a really proper British accent, he went to school in London ... and I remember I wanted to write him a note in Farsi, but I didn't know what his name was [in Farsi].[51] I found it problematic to put down Eddie on the note. I finally looked up what his name was and he did have a Persian name and I wrote that on the note but I don't know if he recognized it. I don't know if he reads Farsi or if he recognized his own name, because I didn't recognize my own name until a year and a half ago.

He continues to explain,

There is [another] guy from DC, out of the Iranians, who we considered the most American because he wasn't born in Iran like the rest of us. Out of all of us, he was probably the only one who is born here ... culturally he doesn't recognize the same things as we recognize, we talk about *Noruz*, he recognizes the concept but not the events that we always associate with it. And like when I say I am going with my parents to a function in Boston there is going to be a singer there or something, he doesn't always recognize those sorts of things ... we always considered him to be the most American but it turns out that he speaks the best Farsi because there is a tight Persian-American community in DC and they speak Farsi a lot whereas the rest of us who have lived in America we're scattered, there are only a dozen people I know who I can speak Farsi to on a regular basis, whereas he had a community to go to, like go to the *cholo kababee* to speak Farsi, or go to stores, we never had that. And so to speak Farsi is really problematic to us because we define him as the most American out of us but he holds language in a way that we don't.

For most, Farsi was the cultural vehicle by which these second-generation Iranians held onto the Iranian culture. All of the participants, with the exception of one male Armenian Iranian, spoke Farsi at a conversational level. Almost none could declare that they write or read Farsi. Thus the language is only held on to orally, but represents a tenuous connection to culture for these students.

The majority of Muslim-Iranians I interviewed had attended Farsi classes, more so than the other religious-ethnic groups. Again, for Muslim-Iranians, knowing Farsi was closely tied to understanding Iranian culture.

> Well, the biggest thing first of all is definitely language, the biggest thing I think is Farsi so had I not gone to Farsi class that part would be lost and that's huge. Like I know a couple of *irooni's* up at Dartmouth who like don't speak any Farsi and like there is a difference there. If you can't ... speak, I feel there's a difference.

Vestiges of an Iranian culture lingered in all participants, in one way or another. Mixed in their new surroundings of American life, these components were adopted by second-generation Iranian students as their Iranian culture.

Right of the Hyphen: American

On the other side of the landscape, the students live their every day lives in an American context. Culture, then, is created inside and outside of the family. Their sense of being an Iranian-American, neither one nor the other, was also created by their contact with their peers, by their schools, and by the media. The media, in particular, cast a dark shadow over their sense of culture. Unanimously, these second-generation Iranians felt that Iranians were portrayed as "terrorists." They felt images were negative not only in the news but also in popular media such as in the movie *Not Without My Daughter*, based on the 1978

book by Betty Mahmoody.[52] Several participants described
the film as influencing how their high school peers saw
their Iranian culture.

> I remember one day she was at my house and *Not
> Without My Daughter* came out and she asked,
> 'does your dad do this?' I was really hurt and really
> offended and I remember it really scarred me. And I
> told my mom 'can you believe it?' I just thought
> how could she think that my father would abuse me
> or hit me or take me away you know. I was really
> offended and I think that scarred my friendships.

Despite a prevalent negative image, these students still
considered themselves American in many respects – a
belief that was often stated with ambivalence, and
sometimes with confusion. When discussing their lives in
the American context, the issue that was often raised, again
but from a different perspective, was the issue of language.
These youth felt most comfortable with the English
language. And it was their ability to use the English
language that separated them from their parents. In terms of
their education, this schism often became an academic
hurdle since they could not seek help from their parents, as
the following two quotes illustrate.

> I couldn't go back to my mom and dad to read
> something or pronounce something or tell me a
> definition. It was the opposite. My sister and I
> would have to, you know, it was the reverse. My
> dad would say, [delete name], how would you say
> this, I would have to tell him. It wasn't the other
> way around. It was pretty much like that always.
> With papers, I couldn't ask my dad, dad could you
> proofread this?

> Language was a big problem especially with my
> parents. Their English is understandable but it's a
> very basic English. So when I'd speak to them, I'd

have to speak 'down' to them, in the same way that they'd have to speak down to me when they spoke Farsi. When it came down to the SATs I took out the SAT books, I memorized about 2000 words, you know word for word, I never heard half the words, I was never much of a reader then either so language was definitely a problem, especially English.

Even though English may have posed some communication challenges within the family, participants felt that their parents promoted the acquisition of the English language. If they were to succeed in the American society, they were told by their parents, it was important that they master the English language. Mastering English, to them, would be academically and economically more advantageous. The command of the English language was not equated with cultural assimilation; rather English was structural assimilation.

Consistently, participants remarked how their parents promoted structural assimilation but not cultural assimilation. Abandoning Farsi for the sake of English for these students was not an issue of cultural assimilation. Rather, issues of cultural assimilation came to the fore around social issues, such as relations with peers and/or dating.

In high school there is so much peer pressure, so much going on. Americans are able to do so many things because they grew up in a different society. But, as an Iranian, your parents raise you with the same mentality that they were raised with even though they're living in a totally different culture so it's really hard to adapt and it's really hard to really be good friends with a lot of American people 'cause they would be able to go out on the weekends and go to parties and ... even pool parties which I wasn't able to go to because my parents were like 'no, you know you can't do that.' And I was like well everybody is going why can't I go?

My parents had certain rules for us and my friends didn't understand. Like I was never allowed to sleep over a friend's house and they were like, "why don't your parents trust us?" It was just hard to explain that it was just a cultural thing, you know. Or school dances. Like I wasn't allowed to go to them and it wasn't so much that I wanted to go to them but it was hard to tell your friends because there weren't any other Iranian girls in my high school, it was hard to get the point across.

Dating, for example, is a salient feature of American college life – but a concept that these students felt clashed with their family values. The links to this clash between their families values of dating and that of their own were often traced back to their younger days. Nearly all the subjects pointed out that they didn't understand why their parents did not allow them to participate in sleepovers with their friends – which all their peers were doing. Socially, these students told me, their parents did not want to assimilate towards the American culture – a culture they felt would steer them away from advancing academically. The following female Muslims shared these thoughts:

My parents when I was younger said when you're fourteen, when I turned fourteen they said sixteen and then I turned sixteen they said no, wait until you are in college. And now I'm in college my mom is saying why aren't you dating!

I think it's fine, everyone should just do it. I wasn't allowed to – ever. I don't know if I still am (laugh) but I think I mean living in America I think you have to because I know I don't want to marry someone straight from Iran and so I would like to marry an Iranian who was brought up in America that's ideal. If I don't find some one who is an Iranian I'll just marry an American. I think it's pretty important to have those sorts of dating skills or just sort of like anything else to be at par with society. So we're not out of it (laugh).

If two people are seen walking together, it's automatically assumed they are dating which I think is very strange. It shouldn't be that way. I think people should be able to go out, I think it's more healthy.

On the topic of dating, gender bias cut across all four religious-ethnicities, and was the sharpest divide among Mashadi Jews. In the following passage, I ask a male Mashadi about the difference he sees between himself and his sisters:

It's okay for me to date. For me, okay, not for my sisters, to date like Americans or like whatever as long as they are Jewish. Even the dating would be shady if I were to date a Catholic girl you know what I mean. I'm being totally candid with you right now. It's perfectly okay for me to do that. I had an American girlfriend for several years but as far as my parents were concerned it's okay for me to date them but 'don't ever think about marrying them, go out and have your fun.' They were accepting because she was Jewish. They're like go have your fun, get it out of your system, but don't ever think of marrying anyone outside of Persian, specifically our particular [Mashadi] community.

So you said it's different for your sisters?

Yeah, absolutely. It's not okay for them to date. Unless my older sister is at that point to see someone, but that's in a totally different sense, seeing them, like do you know the expression, *"Daran rah meeran"*? In Persian, they are walking, that means they are seeing each other, mostly it has a connotation for marriage. You know for *khastegaree* [engagement proposal], whatever. That is what's okay for my sister to do at this age. But no way to date, or to hang out with American guys.

A female Jew explained her point of view on the restrictions on dating:

There are double standards of not being able to go out whereas like your older brother. Girls get a reputation and they can't be seen and they can't you know do certain things because they have to get married. Our parents feel that between the ages of 17 and 21 when you are an undergraduate that's not the time to be dating.

Some students admitted that they were attracted, or gravitated towards the American college scene but that they had pulled themselves back towards their "culture" which in effect was their family-created culture and point of reference. In this family-created culture, education was paramount in respect to their core values.

I am trying not to let go of who I am … the family thing. It took me four years of being here to appreciate those things. In some aspects you have no choice, you just conform but I think I haven't let go of my culture and I am not trying to conform to society.

Several participants drew upon the analogy of the dinner table to explain the shift towards the American culture. As they became more "American" they explained, they spent less time at the dinner table; they had their own "independent" schedules to keep. It was the shift from the importance of community to one's independence that marked their shift towards to the American culture.

The Hyphenated American

I consider myself an American; I do not consider myself Persian. I mean heritage wise I am Persian but I consider myself an American kid. It's really weird because I know what's inside me, my beliefs and everything and the person that I am in the inside is a Persian. I know my values are Persian but I'm an American so it's an interesting mix .... It's a paradox.

I don't feel like I should use the term "assimilated" 'cause that implies you've given up some aspect of your culture but maybe that is the right word, to some degree. I mean we went to school, we did all the same stuff in high school as American kids, like we went to proms, went out on Friday nights ... but I can't say we have assimilated. Assimilate, I feel, is like blended in. Even though I feel we have blended in, I don't really know where to draw the line. To say that like we've given up aspects of *Irooni* culture to mix into the American culture or vice versa, I don't know where I would draw the line, it's like how far ... how far I've gone.

I feel I don't have any true connection to America and no true connection to Iran. I'm like in the middle 'cause I'm raised here but I'm not really an American, and I was never raised in Iran but I feel I'm an Iranian. It's confusing.

Where their sense of selves fell between these two realms – American versus Iranian - was often difficult for even the students themselves to decipher. Most admitted that they had struggled with understanding exactly where they stood between these two worlds. Their sense of confusion often became crystallized in something as supposedly straightforward as their college applications. When they were asked to "categorize" themselves on college applications, many said that a lot of time went into deliberating over the category which best described them. In the following passage I am quizzical as to how and why the participant draws on both her national and religious background. She explains the difficulty and/or "baggage" in choosing one category over another.

I didn't want to say white on my college application, I don't know why, I didn't want to say white. I always thought white was just American and I never thought of myself as an American girl. So I always put down "other." [Laugh] and if there was a line allowing me to explain the other, I'd always put down Persian-Israeli or Israeli-Persian. But my dad would be like what are you doing? [Laugh] and I'd say that's what I am and he said, no, you're white. He would say, it is better for the college -- if they think you were white. And I said, okay but that didn't make sense to me.

Why did he say it's better to say white?

Just because it's less complicated and if you say you're Iranian then they'd be like 'oh well, like stereotyped and stuff' he was afraid like they would start categorizing me. Wait listing me, you know. So he said the simplest thing is to say white. I actually didn't want to do that.

Despite the confusion or frustration about placing themselves in one versus another race/ethnic category, the process of making such a choice forced them to think about their identity. This decision-making process often reinforced their connection to their family and reaffirmed their point of reference, and their culture assumed a position in relation to, though different from, being an American. Here, understanding that their identities were not fully American meant that they were able to draw from another culture to motivate or propel them to advance themselves academically. For example, in the following quote, this male Armenian explains the "hollowness" with just identifying oneself as "American." He saw a distinct advantage to having a culture with which he could associate himself. He said:

> I see it as something you can identify yourself with, you're not just an American; there is more to you than that. There is more to you than just being American. There is a lot of advantages to it, you network, you meet people who share the same beliefs as you do. I want my kids to go to an Armenian school just so they can get that Armenian reinforcement so they can get some sort of a historical cultural background and I think it's important for them to understand their ancestry. They first need a strong base of the Armenian culture. They need that Armenian base first. They can get the American culture from anything. So they wouldn't lose the touch. Because I see Americans they're just carefree. I ask them what are you or who are you, I'm American that's it. Not you're not. You're something. No one is just American. It just seems that Americans don't have the culture that I'm used to. They don't understand that you should not give up your past.

I should note, however, that their sense of self-identity varied across the ethnic-religious categories and was often defined by context. For example, all the Bahá'í - and Jewish-Iranians in this study referred to themselves as Persian. Moreover, in all references to the country and the culture, they used the words Persia and Persian respectively, never Iran. Though a small semantic difference, it reveals a window into the culture with which they identified themselves. Members of these two modern-day persecuted groups in Iran associated more with Iran's past than with its present. Even the Muslim participants flipped between using Iran and Persia; the latter was used in conjunction with a sense of pride.

> Persia has more history. I think of people with pride. When people were proud to be Persian and there wasn't a stigma.

Jewish-Iranians, specifically, communicated another layer of association. Not only did they want to identify themselves with Persia as opposed to Iran, but they also mentioned that they identified with being a Jew in America rather than just an American. Paradoxically, even though the two combined gave them a double-minority identity it served to strengthen their position in relation to a perceived negative American culture.

> I'm a Jew before I'm a Persian. You know it's like a double minority. The two of them has both affected me and I can't really explain to what extent, in what way [silence]. [Judaism] gave us another way to identify ourselves with a larger group, while I'm not sure being a Muslim Iranian helped them identify with other people. But definitely being a Jewish Iranian gave us just another thing to latch on to.

> Jewish, Iranian, American. All three, there are three things that really make me who I am; it's not that I am Jewish when I go to the synagogue; it's not that I'm Iranian when I speak Persian; it's like these parts that make me but I can't say which is more important. But I'm definitely all three of them, no matter what order you put them in.

Many explained how their names are at the center of their definition of their identity as well as their struggle with it. For instance, this female Jewish participant explains that her name is part and parcel of a three-pronged cultural identity:

> [I]t's not completely who I am but I guess I have my middle name, [name deleted] that is my Jewish name and my last name that's Iranian and my first name is American!

Names also provided a hanger on which they could hang their cultural identity: a sense of being unique in the American culture. One female Armenian participant told me,

> I enjoy my first name, it was unique even though there are a lot of Armenians with the same name, I enjoy my first name. I didn't want to be another Susie or Jane. My name definitely gave me my identity. I've always been the only [name deleted] anywhere so everyone always knew me. People remember you because your name is unique.

But sometimes, when wanting to blend into their American identity, their names brought attention they could otherwise have done without. One female participant explained that during her college interview, the admissions officer asked her about her name, a question, which in her opinion was getting to her background (and religion). Reticent, reluctant and frustrated she answered him and explains what transpired:

> He asked where are your parents from. I think people usually do that because I speak fluent English and I don't have an accent or anything. So he asked that and then he asked what religion I was! I was like this is an illegal question but he's the dean of admissions so what am I supposed to do? So I'm like well, yeah, I'm Muslim. Then he said,

"you must be following the Egypt Air Crash thing pretty closely" (laugh). And I was like well, as closely as anyone else. What are you trying to say? And he went on to talk about suppression of women in Muslim societies and everything, and whatever.

What seemed unfair to her was that being identified as an Iranian, a Muslim, and being associated with terrorism had captured the disadvantages of being a minority but yet, in reality, she has no legal recourse as a minority in this country. Appropriately, she called this, "the double-edged sword of being an Iranian." Another participant, a male Bahá'í had a similar experience:

Iranians are classified as white Caucasians but people would look at me [deducing from my dark features] and treat me as a minority. For example, I applied for this scholarship -- I interviewed for it they loved me, but I didn't get one award or scholarship at all, nothing. What happened was that they categorized the applications according to whites and minorities. My friend who was black and had all lower grades than me got so much money from the school. The category of white damaged my chances of being picked for it. If I were a minority then I would have gotten that money. It was a financial and academic based decision yet it was based on race. My mom was working three jobs and she was making like $11,000 a year. I'll never forget that. It was a bitter memory.

American life, for example, stresses independence and freedom of choice; while they felt the Iranian culture stresses dependence (to family and community) and is bounded by restrictions (to status, for example). The combination of the two gives them a superior advantage, particularly when it comes to their education. One female Muslim participant said, "I have the best of the two worlds.

I have the opportunities this country has to offer; and I have my culture." But the balance between the two "worlds" is not as easy as she describes it. For some, there was considerable tension between the two.

Tension between the two realms were strongest and most noticeable for those trying the hardest to stay close to the elements they believe constitute Iranian culture. The clearest example of the conflict between these realms is evinced among the Mashadi-Jews as they openly discuss how the family needs to remain the strongest force within the lives of the new generation. Nowhere in my interviews was this more clearly demonstrated than in an essay one participant sent to me as a way of "educating" me about the reality of the cultural forces in her life. In her essay, she wrote:

Knowing well the behaviors and tendencies of my community, a favorite high school teacher of mine once warned me to move away from home and the Mashadis as soon as I had turned eighteen. I was tempted to take her advice many times during my junior and senior years of high school; however, I could never bring myself to run away. There was always something holding me back and restoring me to my senses. I now realize that even then, I knew that by leaving home and completely "Americanizing," I would miss my family and the security with which they provided me. I would not be able to live without Friday night dinners or weekly visits to my grandparents' house. Overall, although I have had horrible past experiences with the Mashadis ... and although I will always be rebellious towards the community, I know that the culture and traditions of the Iranian Jews are too precious to be lost or forgotten.

Her sentiments resonated in all my interviews with Mashadi Jews; apparently it was also part of their community discussion. One exasperated Mashadi Jew talks about the tension in a *Megillah*[53] editorial:

> Where else, in the past, were our children exposed to so much drugs, sex, and alcohol? Where did our youth learn to force teenagers to drink shots of alcohol in order to be able to enter a private party? Where did our youngsters lose respect for each other and learn to take sexual advantage of one another? Did our teens want to have annual fashion shows before we moved to Great Neck? .... If there is anyone to blame for anything wrong that happens to our children, it is the parents. We have been so preoccupied with trying to get established here that we have been ignoring our children's needs (Etessami, 2000).

According to one male Muslim participant in this study, there is indeed a lot of pressure in the American social scene towards potentially negative behavior. However, he explained how he learned to be "Iranian" in the social settings he encounters:

> When you are in a club and there is drinking around you, there is drugs around you, there is dancing, there is interaction with women, you don't do the wrong thing, you choose in your mind what is appropriate as an Iranian and you take care of it and that's how you maintain your "Iranian-ness" even though you are an American, or you are in the American society. I don't know any Iranians that don't drink. None of us are devout Muslims, pray, fast, or not drink. So in that way, we are all pretty much Americanized.

In the same way that he explained how he used his sense of being an Iranian, most described their ability to rise above the prejudices and stereotyping that they sensed existed in the American society. Even though they might have been confused as to exactly what constitutes the Iranian culture, they were certainly sure that it was a culture that was far superior to the American culture. One participant said, "the American culture is the lack of culture." Repeatedly, the comparison between the American and the Iranian culture was that the former lacked depth, lacked history, while the latter was "culturally rich." Identifying with the latter, then, was more positive than associating with the former. By the mere fact that their families were from another culture, they felt they had an identity that was far more unique and historically rooted than average Americans. This gave them a sense of self-esteem that was untiringly tested against a pervasive negative media stereotype. One female participant who grew up in Texas, and whose father had lost his business as a result of the anti-Iranian sentiment of the early 1980s described the tension she felt with the American society:

> My dad's business was located in [name deleted], this is very small town in Texas, with a predominantly white population ... you know, blue collar folks and farms, and houses that were acres away from each other. It just so happened that whatever happened in the Middle East, regardless of our nationality, people began to express their hate -- in the form of vandalism ... and decreased business ... many of our loyal customers began going to our competitors.... and slowly, our business began to sink, no profit, too many losses... and soon, employees began to drop like flies....forcing us to work there as a family... we went from being accepted to becoming the outcasts...and "terrorists" to the town... we knew what needed to be done and that was to leave...

Another female Muslim said that she felt that the stereotypes of Iranians are as strong as ever in the American society. She states:

I don't think they will ever accept us. I don't think
they'll accept us until someone comes out and
discovers something, like does the world a great
favor. Let's say if I came out and I cured heart
disease and being an Iranian I don't think anyone
will accept me until that day. I don't think they'll
accept our people and our culture until something
like that happens. I don't think until we have like a
surgeon general or someone leading the country that
we'll be accepted. I think they associated us with
terrorism.

Interestingly, they did not internalize negative
stereotypes, believing it was the American people's
ignorance. Instead, the prevalent stereotypes were used
constructively. In a sense, these youth served as what I saw
as "cultural diplomats."

We like letting people know we are Iranian, we're
proud of being Iranian, rather we're proud of being
Persian. We recognize that people have views
which we don't agree with on Iran, and what we try
to define all the things that we think are good about
Iranian culture and share that with other people....
It's about saying this is our food, this is what we
eat, well, not this is what we eat, but what we eat
when we go to restaurants, and when we are
dancing, this is how we dance, and you are trying to
share that with people who aren't Iranian, not try to
define that you are all the same but it's really
something that helps explain you to other people
and we try to educate them about things. ... I mean
most of it is you are trying to show that this is the
good about the Persian culture.

I always tell my friends about [Iran]. I think people
always stereotype Iranians.... and so I've got a lot
of books about Iran and pictures I always show my
friends and they're always like 'wow, that's Iran, I

always thought it was a desert!' I try to make them aware.

When asked why they felt compelled to promote Iran, one male Muslim said that he was not promoting Iran. Rather, he was using the culture to promote himself. This self-promotion was always closely tied to a social context that publicizes negative stereotypes of Iranians.

It's not really representing the goodness of Iran but of you. It's different from you defending the culture or culture promoting you. I don't think I have to take the role of being a statesman of Iran and saying yeah Iran is good but I like what is Iranian in me. And I am using culture to define me and using culture to help me out and I think whenever someone says something disparaging about Iran I think about the Iranians that I know, I know they are successful and educated so I just think the person is confused.

The extent to which these second-generation Iranians strove to show the positive side of the Iranian culture even manifested in the interviewing process. One male Jewish Iranian only discussed the negative aspects of what he considered the "Iranian culture" after the interview was "formally" completed. It was as though, what they wanted to present about their sense of being an Iranian had to be positive.

Both their desires to be positive and open about being an Iranian were far different than their parents, the majority of whom experienced the backlash of the hostage crisis. For example, one female Muslim participant who grew up in California commented on the difference between her attitude and her parents' attitude of being an Iranian:

My brother and I were always so proud; we were always like "Iran, Iran, Iran." But my mom used to say "don't say you're Iranian, I mean if people ask you of course say you are Iranian but don't be so open about it." I think they lived in the era when people were really distrustful to Iran and you know my mom would tell me how they would burn Iranian flags and people would be chanting during the whole hostage crisis. They really felt scared to be Iranian. So when I told them there was an international fair and I was wearing my Iran tee-shirt with a flag on it she was like, "I can't believe you did that!" Yeah, they were hesitant about saying they're Iranian.

Several Iranian students said they wear Iranian emblem t-shirts, hang posters of Iran in their college fraternity and sorority bedrooms, and dine with their friends at *cholo-kababees* (traditional Iranian restaurants), all in an effort to acquire an identity that "I am not an American." Being an American, or losing their Iranian culture, was associated with losing their values, for behaving in ways that were not socially acceptable with Iranians. One male Muslim participant used such examples: keeping family issues within the family, lack of feelings/emotions, respecting elders, or even saying "salaam" (good morning) to your family when you wake up. He said, "whatever I did wrong was always associated with the fact that I was more American and I kind of believe that myself." The consensus was that Americans lacked respect, especially for their family members. For example, one participant said:

I guess the way kids treat their parents the way parents treat their kids it's totally different, there's no respect at all, either way the parents or the kids or the kids and the parents.

Respecting the family and the culture of the family was important. Familial and cultural dynamics as highly interrelated forces forged a strong factor in their educational impressions and experiences.

Socioeconomic Status

Most of the Iranian Bahá'ís I know escaped. They came here after the revolution so a lot of them had to escape. They didn't come with much; they didn't come here with money or carpets or anything. And they had to leave their friends behind, their families behind, all of their possessions, everything they gained in Iran, everything -- they had to leave it all behind. I mean our family came here with one suitcase and no job, nothing. My mom had a high school diploma from Iran, and my dad worked for an oil company in Iran so he came here with no language skills -- nothing to show. So it was very hard. When we started out, we lived in an apartment that had two bedrooms. It was small. Somehow they managed, you know. A lot hard work. It wasn't in a bad neighborhood but now we live in [neighborhood name deleted] -- it's an upper-scale neighborhood and they have a very nice house and very nice cars and they send their kids to Boston University -- an expensive university.

Various data sources (e.g., Census Data and Consumer Price Index) have characterized first generation Iranian immigrants as educationally and economically at a par with, or above average, as compared to the average native-born white United States citizen. They have also been considered as the third most highly educated immigrant group (after Asian Indians and Taiwanese). Yet, eight of the thirty students in this study (3 Muslim; 2 Armenian; and 3 Bahá'ís) described their families socioeconomic status different than the one that has generally typified Iranians – that of being affluent. As the above quote illustrates, for example, many of the Bahá'í Iranians had to leave Iran with little resources other than the ones they could place in a suitcase. They sold their homes and borrowed money to purchase their tickets to the United States.

These students also revealed that it was important for their families to display an outward appearance (*zaher*) that they were not struggling financially. One students' remarks poignantly captures their desire of creating the appearance of "having it" even to their own children:

> My mom told me that when we first came here they used to take us to Toys-R-Us. My mom and dad would drink some coffee in the mall and my brother and I used to go in there and just play. But we would never buy anything. I guess they were buffering us so we wouldn't feel that we didn't have as much as the other kids. That we had a *kambood* [lack of]; that we didn't feel like we were less than anyone else.

The importance of creating the illusion of being financially well off was essentially sending a message to outsiders -- and their own children: we are at par with the rest.

In terms of the effects of family socioeconomics on their education, I found that regardless of their family's background, they held similar views on the importance of education. For example, several of my participants had parents who worked three jobs, worked in factories, and/or were unemployed for lengths of time. Yet, their attitude towards obtaining an education, their educational experiences, and their ability to perform academically were equal to their fellow Iranians whose parents were surgeons and doctors. That is to say, among these second-generation Iranians, there was no difference between those who had the benefits of family income and those who did not. Education was important regardless of their family's socioeconomic status.

Although, initially I was tempted to conclude that socioeconomic status did not play a role in the educational experiences of these second-generation youth, I realized that I was only considering socioeconomic status as a predictor of their education. Instead, socioeconomic status motivated these students to aspire to do well academically. My subsequent formulation was that status was indeed important – not as something that had prepared them to do well educationally, rather as something that motivated them to do well. The implicit message coming through these interviews was that education was important because it enabled them to acquire a coveted social status, which I explain below.

<u>"Social Signal of Achievement"</u>

While second-generation Iranians in this sample admitted that their pursuit of education rested highly on their desire to ascertain socioeconomic status, they stressed that their educational degrees were relevant in another way – as a "social signal of achievement." And, in many ways this social signal of achievement was more important to them than its related counterpart, socioeconomic status. That is to say, for example, most of these second-generation Iranians, with the exception of Iranian Mashadi Jews, often preferred to obtain a medical degree more than acquiring financial wealth because with their educational titles they gained respect and acceptance. Mashadi-Jews thought that economic status is much more important than having academic credentials. Within the Mashadi Jewish community, financial status was inextricably tied to social status; achieving the former would guarantee the latter. Among Muslim and Bahá'ís, I found that they would prefer to have higher academic credentials than to amassing wealth (though having money was very important to them, they would prioritize the two as such). Armenians swayed, placing importance on both, neither one nor the other.

Teachers & Peers: What Was Irrelevant

None of the participants in this study referred to any of their teachers, past or present, as having influenced them in positive ways. Sadly, more remembered instances where their teachers had humiliated either their background or their names. Many believed that their experiences were tied to the political context of the 1980s, when negative images of Iran were rampant in the American society.

> I think the 80's were a nightmare, kids making fun of me, I was the only Iranian kid EVER until I got to college. Ever! I had this teacher who called me Salami, it was horrible. So everyone else called me Salami after that. Or they would say it in a way, like "Oh, [name deleted], where are you from?" I'd say I'm from Iran and they'd be like "Oh, you're from Iran" (in a shocked way). One day a kid came up to me and said my dad said you guys are murdering Americans.

Participants remarked that nowadays their younger siblings in schools do not face the same hostility.

Intriguingly, many participants said that if their teachers made a negative reference to Iran, they would try their hardest to proved them wrong. In many instances I noticed that students used their family's point of reference to contest their teachers' negative impressions.

> Once a teacher said something about the Persian Empire – like, 'imagine if the Persian empire had taken over we would all be in the dark ages' or something. So I wrote this paper about how the Persian Empire is one of the best influences ... I think it kind of makes you work harder to prove them wrong. I always try to do my best in front of those teachers 'cause they knew I'm Iranian and I didn't want to give a bad, you know, I wanted to leave a good impression so they would not think she's just a typical you know Iranian, whatever their stereotypes were.

> My freshman year in high school, in my history class, I don't know what we were studying but we

got off the topic and we started talking about Iran and how its people were living ... I don't know but it was this horrible image of Iran. It's hard because when you are a student you want to respect what your teacher says so I'd go home and say 'mom, I know this isn't the case' and she'd say 'of course not.'

There were situations like [the teachers] would talk about the revolution and would say things that made me feel uncomfortable. Or like they talk about the TWA incident and I just felt uncomfortable because my friends knew that I was Iranian and the teacher knew and I could feel the tension. I just felt uncomfortable. I would just wish they would teach things in a different way -- that not all Iranians are the same way, they would assume that everyone is the same.

The above quotes illustrate the residual anti-Iranian sentiments with which second-generation Iranians continued to occasionally come into contact. Even though they are sentiments hurled against Iran as a nation, these individuals felt the personal destruction apparent beneath them.

The majority of participants believed that they did not receive any attention from their teachers because they were not "problem students" or that they did well enough not the gain their attention. One female participant captures it as such: "They didn't notice it because I always was self-determined." In sum, there was no reason why teachers should signal them out – they did their work and they blended in.

In terms of peers, interviews revealed that peers were described as varying academically – some as being better students and some poorer students. And, none believed that their friends had influenced them in terms of their education. Instead, their peers were a respite between their

family environment and their daily lives in the American
context. Even though my subjects recalled instances when
growing up their peers ridiculed them, as the below quote
illustrates, they appeared as comments made because they
were different as immigrants; not necessarily derision
based on their Iranian backgrounds.

> I remember there was a time when a lot of my
> friends were playing in our driveway and my
> grandmother came out and she said something in
> Farsi and I answered her ... she came out just in the
> front porch, front steps, and said something like you
> have a telephone call. And one of the kids was like,
> "I didn't know you spoke Chinese." And they
> laughed. I felt different.

Being different, in effect, became the single most
striking reason with which they described "kids their age."
When it came to their friendships, however, the common
descriptor was that they were children of immigrants as
well and/or they had had international experience.

> My peers? Definitely minority. I think we all relate
> to each other. We're all second-generation. My
> really close friend right now, her parents don't
> speak English. They're from Peru. Her parents are
> like mine, but hers are more dependent on her; they
> rely on her. I guess when we exchange stories of
> how it was like to be growing up, we could relate.
> And I have another friend who is Israeli. She came
> here when she was very young and her parents only
> speak Hebrew. But definitely my friends are
> minorities. I have one friend who is white but it's
> weird how I find the same type of friends. Her
> parents never graduated from high school, they
> struggled and just now they are going back to get
> their GED.

My American friends know about the international scene, you know, they are global, they know where Iran is on the map, or they know the history or if they don't they are willing to understand or learn about it. They're not closed people, they are not like America is number one.

Many participants mentioned that they did not usually have other Iranian friends.

I think you can learn a lot more, and it's more positive to be in a diverse group rather than a homogeneous group. So I think being around people of different cultures it's more lively and you can gain more from it because you learn. You don't become stagnant in one area. I mean like at BU I mean I have friends who are Iranian but I don't only hang around with Iranians.

My problem is that I don't have that many friends that are Iranian. There is no body like that in my school and I went to the Persian classes they used to be held here at [name of institution] but now they're in Watertown. I used to go to those but it didn't seem like anybody there wanted to have a friendship with another Iranian.

Whether not having Iranian friends was by choice or by the virtue of their physical distance to other second-generation Iranians, it shed light on several issues. There was often the conflict between the Iranian culture that their families espoused and that of the broader community of Iranians in which they lived. This issue points to the diversity among Iranians and how being an "Iranian" often can be very different amongst those in the community. Coming into contact with other Iranians, then, often meant that they had to draw upon their vague sense of the Iranian culture. Also, being with other nationalities re-emphasized their sense of being the "other" in relation to the American culture but did not force them to be the connoisseur of the culture with which they were identifying. And, perhaps most importantly, maintaining Iranian peers would have drawn attention to them.

> Anyone I was with was non-Iranian pretty much. Any friends that I made were non-Iranians. I couldn't form a group of Iranians and just be with them, not that I necessarily wanted to. Like I think that with the Asian groups, the immigrant Asian groups, they stayed amongst themselves and they didn't encourage the language. They weren't assimilated. I think you can learn a lot more in a diverse group than in a homogeneous group.

In sum, these second-generation Iranians wanted to "blend in" when it came to their schooling. They chose peer groups that facilitated that process. Whether or not there were Iranians around in their schools, the majority of these students felt that they would deliberately choose not to associate with only Iranians.

CHAPTER FIVE

Family, Culture, and Status

Second-generation Iranian students in my sample, as I described in the previous chapter, deemed family, culture, and their desire to acquire status as the most important factors in helping shape their personal and educational experiences. These factors varied across many dimensions, including their religious and ethnic orientation, or depending on when their families migrated to the United States. Moreover, I found that each factor is highly interrelated with its two other counterparts. In this chapter, though they are closely interrelated, I explore each theme independently to gain a better sense of how each operated within the lives of second-generation Iranians.

First, there is the concept of family – its structure and its relations within that structure. Within a variety of structural and relational dynamics, Iranian families were able to nurture a "point of reference" for second-generation Iranians, who for the most part had never been to Iran and whose only conception of the country came through their families' tales, pictures, and renditions of Iran. Second-generation Iranians gained a sense of responsibility for their education because of the educational autonomy their families bestowed upon them. They appreciated the opportunity to make their own choices regarding their education; they felt that, in this sense, they had the respect of their family. Conversely, this group of second-generation Iranians respected their family heritage and their parents' struggles to provide them with educational opportunities. This mutual respect is the basis of what can be considered a form of family discipline.

Second, there is the concept of "culture." Second-generation Iranians in this study combined two cultures – Iranian and American – through a strategy of structural and cultural assimilation. This group of Iranians, for instance, exemplifies the issue of language acquisition not as a process of cultural assimilation, but as one of structural assimilation.

Finally, there is the duality of socioeconomic status – both as a predictor and as an impetus for their educational experiences. The latter was more relevant: high socioeconomic status inspired second-generation Iranians to earn degrees in order to become professionals and achieve high socioeconomic status.

Family

Finding that family played a crucial role in the educational experiences of these second-generation students is not surprising. Family structure and the relationships within the family are common predictors of academic performance. Many studies have found that positive educational outcomes are associated with families in which parents foster the values of education, achievement, and motivation (Ekstrom, Goertz, Pollack, & Rock, 1986; Hernandez, 1993; Rumberger, 1983).

Indeed, family structure can play an important role, but that structure varies widely among immigrant families, due to a host of factors, such as the conditions that immigrants encounter when they arrive in a new country and their particular cultural background. Kinship becomes an issue of support, or "social security," among immigrant families

(Bateson, 2000; Foner, 1997; Pérez, 1996). Iranians, like other immigrants, had their own definition of the term "family" and other basic, taken-for-granted cultural aspects of kinship, like who is considered a relative. For some, "family" consisted of one parent; for others the family unit was comprised of the nuclear family; for Jewish Iranians, family extended to the community; and for many family included Iranian family friends who had taken on the role of extended family (or as I call them in this study, these friends became "pseudo-families) in the United States. By expanding the structure of the family, Iranian families were able to expand effectively the web of educational support that existed for second-generation Iranians.

Family relations and dynamics also played an important part in shaping the educational experience of second-generation Iranians. Generally, among immigrant families, generational gaps are intensified as parents and children identify with contrasting cultures and languages (Ima, 1995). Conflicts surrounding family relations have been identified and described among many immigrant groups, including Mexicans, Haitians, Jamaicans, Filipinos, Punjabis, and Koreans. Similar generation gaps were also evident among Iranian families in this study. For instance, the children of these Iranian immigrants were able to adapt to the new language and culture of the host country more easily than their parents. Yet, these noticeable gaps did not weaken the educational zeal that these students possessed. Although second-generation Iranians questioned their parents' views of American culture, and despite the growing differences between themselves and their parents, they were able to keep their commitment to education.

While family structures varied widely among Iranian families of various religious-ethnicities, and while relations within them were often questioned by second-generation Iranians, three characteristics consistently emerged as salient features of the Iranian family environment: point of reference, autonomy, and respect. These elements gave them a powerful sense of who they were: they understood that they had a proud heritage and that they had a responsibility to their families to make the most of their education in this country.

Point of Reference

Suárez-Orozco and Suárez-Orozco (1995) refer to the ability of first-generation immigrants to orient themselves to their place of origin as "dual frame of reference." They state that "immigrants constantly compare and contrast their current lot in the host society with their previous lives"(p. 53). Generally, through firsthand experience, first-generation immigrants could compare their earlier and present lives and feel better off in the new country than in their country of origin.

Second-generation Iranians, however, possessed a similar ability: while they had never been to Iran or left at a very early age, they could still use the "dual frame of reference" to compare their lives here with those at home. They did not have memories of Iran to compare to their daily lives, since they had not spent time growing up there. Rather, they developed a sense of the duality from their parents' memories and stories. Because their ability to make such comparisons was based on what they heard from their parents, and not on their own experiences, I distinguish it as being a "point of reference." Amazingly, their parents helped create this duality for their children despite the fact that their children never lived in Iran. Bateson (2000) describes how Iranians look back on their lives in Iran, in a description that is emotionally potent and similar to much of what these second-generation Iranians heard from their parents: "...the smells of rice cooking, of the walled courtyard cooled and wetted down for the evening, the taste of fresh bread and herbs, the constant back-and-forth to the homes of relatives" (p.119). These descriptions evoke a sense of belonging, of family, of warmth. But, second-generation Iranians embraced far more than their parents' nostalgic recollection of their lives back in Iran. Their understanding of Iran was also rooted in a deep sense of its history: for second-generation Iranian Jews, Iran was where their ancestors had lived for over two thousand years; for Iranian Bahá'ís it was where their faith had emerged; and for Muslim Iranians it was a cultural heritage rich with contributions in the arts, sciences, and philosophy. Thus, their family's daily lives – feelings of warmth, family, and togetherness -- fused with the tremendous pride that second-generation Iranians took in their historic ethnic origin to create a point of reference for themselves.

Concurrently, while families conjured up a positive image of their ethnic origin, they also stressed the opportunities and freedom that their migration had afforded their children. For decades, access to American educational institutions had been prized and coveted by Iranians in a society where only 10 percent of the population had access to institutions of higher education. Even if individuals were fortunate enough to gain acceptance, they could not study what they wanted; rigid placement exams determined their professional trajectory. In Iran's highly class-stratified society, additional education improved one's social and economic status. The combination of limited access and the power of education was ingrained in the first generation of Iranians to come to the United States. And they effectively communicated to their children their complete belief in the value of pursuing it here.

Second-generation Iranians in my sample, then, knew that they had proud roots and that their family was better off – in terms of educational opportunities – in the United States than in Iran. Rather than despair over their fate, they understood that they must take advantage of the possibilities open to them. For many, this was exacerbated by feelings of guilt knowing that their relatives back in Iran could not access the same quality of education. These sentiments conflicted with the negative stereotypes these students experienced in their lives outside the family. The American interpretation of the Iranian culture was exemplified in an American movie, *Not Without My*

Daughter, which exploited Americans' perceptions of Iran after the unrest of the late 1970s and early 1980s. Nearly all the students in my sample made some sort of reference to this movie and how their peers, and even some teachers, understood the Iranian culture as it was represented in this antagonistic movie about Iranians. Second-generation Iranians, feeling that Americans perceived them as terrorists, tried to dispel American stereotypes by working hard academically and by displaying the positive side of their culture (e.g., taking friends to Iranian restaurants, having posters of the Iranian countryside in dormitory rooms, etc.). They were the "cultural diplomats" of a misunderstood and misrepresented culture in American society, and part of that diplomacy meant doing well academically.

Such a negative social context could have had negative educational implications. For example, in similarly disrespected immigrant groups, such as Mexicans and Haitians, students often internalize pejorative social images and consequently fail academically (Suárez-Orozco, 1995; Waters, 1996). These second-generation Iranian students, however, did not internalize negative perceptions. Instead, they pointed to the "ignorance" of the Americans. They could draw upon a rich repertoire of role models (most often family members) and family heritage to protect themselves from internalizing negative impressions, which were available as part of their point of reference, therefore allowing for positive educational results.

Autonomy and Authority

Iranian families realized that their migration to the United States had placed them in a fluid society, where change took place rapidly. Schools, as microcosms of American society, are a gauge of social change. Second-generation Iranians were in a better position than their parents to evaluate their own educational needs, and therefore the parents gave them the autonomy to make their own decisions about their education. Thus these second-generation Iranians became the educational authority within the family structure. While the family provided the point of reference from which they could direct their educational goals, the children were given the authority and autonomy to make their own choices.

Authority as a concept has traditionally been discussed in educational and political arenas in connection with "agencies of social control rather than with agencies of social change and liberation" (Benne, 1970, p. 385). Most conceptions of authority view freedom in opposition to authority, seeing authority as coercive and freedom as meaning independence. However, Benne, a progressive educator from an earlier generation, suggested that authority, particularly educational authority, should be considered differently:

The ultimate bearer of educational authority is a community life in which its subjects are seeking fuller and more valid membership. Actual bearers and subjects of this authority must together build a proximate set of mutual relationships in which the aim is the development of skills, knowledge, values, and commitments which will enable the subjects to function more fully and adequately as participants in a wider community life which lies beyond the proximate educational associations. (Benne, 1970, p. 401)

In the above passage, Benne also suggested that authority should be defined by its relational characteristic, that it is developed in a larger meaningful context, a coherent environment of commitments, and through relationships where subjects have a collective vision. By re-conceptualizing the notion of authority, its role among second-generation Iranians can be understood differently as well. Second-generation Iranians maintained a point of reference -- the perspective of a larger meaningful context – that education was critically important in their lives. There was reciprocity – a collective vision -- between the vision that the family created and their children's desires to achieve educationally.

In essence, the authority that second-generation Iranians had towards their educational decisions was discretionary power, or, rather, educational autonomy. Lipsky (1980) says that in order to use discretionary power, or autonomy, one must be able to see it and then seize it. Lipsky's notion of autonomy captures the ways in which second-generation Iranians understood, or rather "saw," the educational opportunities they had in this country and then "seized" those opportunities through their relentless drive to gain an education.

Moreover, second-generation Iranians maintained a point of reference: they respected the family background and took pride in it. Conversely, the families granted educational autonomy and expected the new generation to make their own educational choices. This is the mutual respect I referred to earlier. In this next section, I explain how these second-generation Iranians prompted me to also re-conceptualize the definition of respect and the ways in which respect formed the basis of family discipline.

These second-generation Iranians respected their families. Many had compassion for the ways their families had struggled to migrate to the United States and the ways by which they had succeeded here. The following is an example of how, through the connection of point of reference, they respected their parents' desires of success for them. In an emotionally tearful comment, a female Muslim explained:

> I'm here [the U.S.] because of my parents. My dad used to tell me, "I want you to have what I couldn't have" [silence -- tears]. My dad broke down in tears one day and said that I want the best for you and [name deleted]; I want you guys to make it; I want you to be happy, I want you to do what you want to do, and I never want you to settle. He was always saying you are in charge of your future.

Conversely, the families trusted their children. They appreciated that their children understood their educational choices better than they could; in return they granted them educational autonomy. An Armenian-Iranian male student, for example, thought that he was in charge of his education, rather than his mother:

> My mother will call me and will ask me what I'm doing and I'll say I'm reading so she'll say good, but it's never what's your work on or how many hours have you put in? I think she has put a lot of trust in myself just because I think she knows that I put that pressure on myself, I put a lot of pressure on myself to succeed.

Respect

The notion of respect and trust have been embedded in the development of moral character (Bennett, 1988; Benninga, 1988; Coles & Genevie, 1990; Durkheim, 1961; Gow, 1989; Power, 1989). Lawrence-Lightfoot (1999) aptly describes how respect has been commonly defined as:

> .... deference to status and hierarchy; as driven by duty, honor, and a desire to avoid punishment, shame, or embarrassment.... Respect is seen as involving some sort of debt due people because of their attained or inherent position, their age, gender, class, race, professional status, accomplishments, etc. (p. 9)

Yet, Lawrence-Lightfoot (1999) provides a counter definition to the traditionally held concept of respect, postulating that "respect creates symmetry, empathy, and connection in all kinds of relationships..." (p. 10). It is in her re-conceptualization of "respect" that the experience of second-generation Iranians rests.

Among Iranians of these two generations, there was mutual respect – the parents recognized that their children understood their own schooling and did not need parental guidance; the children appreciated the autonomy they were afforded to make their own schooling decisions. "Respect generates respect," according to Lawrence-Lightfoot (1999). The presence of respect within their family strengthened the desire and commitment of these second-generation Iranians. It was not "dutiful compliance" to satisfy the wishes of their parents, but their own conviction that nothing was more important than to pursue an education.

In many ways, I consider the mutual respect concept as a powerful form of family (parental) discipline among Iranian families. In her doctoral thesis, Rambaud (1996) discusses how mutual respect is a form of childrearing that downplays the importance of power between parents and children. Through this form of discipline, Iranian families were able to encourage, rather than coerce, their children into believing in the value of their education. This form of discipline is particularly important among immigrant families Rambaud says, since parents "arm children with an understanding of how to rise in the system: to have respect and to gain respectability" (p. 73).

Unfortunately, no studies have been done on the parenting style of Iranian-Americans, and whether the concept of mutual respect is indeed a parenting style among Iranian families living in the United States. I believe, however, that a particular form of parenting was developed as a consequence of migration. Because families entrusted their children to make their own educational choices and since the new generation being reared in the United States maintained a point of reference, there is mutual respect. Hence, mutual respect is a by-product of the transformations that Iranian families experienced through the process of migration.

The Iranian family environment, notwithstanding religious-ethnic differences, nurtured the presence of three distinct factors: point of reference, autonomy, and respect. In the next section, I discuss the role that culture played in the educational experiences of second-generation Iranians.

A generation ago, social scientists believed that immigrants' "ethnic" culture was detrimental to their success in their new host society, America (Glazer, 1954; Warner & Srole, 1945). As the twentieth century drew to a close, their modern-day counterparts contradicted the original view and argued that "ethnic" culture can essentially make immigrants successful members of this society (Caplan, Whitmore, & Choy 1992; Gibson, 1988; Matute-Bianchi, 1986). Second-generation Iranians in my study illuminated a middle ground – that in order to be successful members of American society, the integration of both cultures is necessary. While they found it difficult to find a precise definition for each of these "cultures," their experiences reveal that second-generation Iranians borrowed and adopted from two different cultural realms. Their experiences also illustrate that their blend of the two cultures can be considered in terms of structural and cultural assimilation.

Culture

There has been much confusion and controversy concerning the definition of culture (Jahoda, 1984; Segall, 1986). Its most fundamental definition was provided by: Herkovits (1948), who suggested that culture is the "human-made part" of the environment. Kluckhohn (1944), a classical cultural anthropologist, defined culture as the total way of life of a people, as a way of thinking, feeling, and believing, an abstraction from behavior, and a mechanism regulating behavior. And, Geertz (1973) proposed that we need to find a more theoretical concept of culture – that when studying culture, one should not look for facts and laws, but rather for meaning, and interpretation.

In terms of immigrants, culture is often referred to as either "original" or "ethnic." The terms "original" and "ethnic" refer to the languages, ideas, beliefs, values and behavioral patterns that immigrants bring with them from their homelands (Zhou & Bankston, 1996). Social scientists of mid-twentieth century described as "inferior" those immigrants who could not adapt, or shed their original ethnic culture for mainstream American life (Warner & Srole, 1945). Their formulations equated successful membership in the American society with assimilation to mainstream America. Immigrant culture -- the language, ideas, beliefs, values, behavioral patterns, and all else that immigrants bring with them -- was considered a hindrance to becoming full members of American society. To succeed, immigrants had to "divest themselves of their previous cultural patterns, including their ethnic identification and languages" (Zhou & Bankston, 1996, p. 198; also see Alba & Nee, 1997; Glazer, 1954).

Iranians entered a racially and ethnically pluralistic American society in the late 1970s (Gans, 1992; Pedraza & Rumbaut, 1996; Suárez-Orozco, 2000).[54] As part of the post-1965, or contemporary, immigrant groups, Iranians found that their educational and economic success was no longer dictated along a single path of conformity. Portes (1995) describes "segmented" paths of adaptation in which certain strategies are ultimately associated with success (academic and economic) in American society. Essentially, ethnic group membership and retention of one's ethnic culture, in this case Iranian, can be considered a potential resource rather than (as traditionally believed) a disadvantage (Caplan, Choy, & Whitmore, 1992; Gibson, 1988; Matute-Bianchi, 1986). The increasingly popular explanation of immigrant educational performance has been linked to the cultural values, beliefs, and practices of immigrants (Caplan, Whitmore, & Choy, 1989; Gibson, 1988, 1995; Kao & Tienda, 1995; Matute-Bianchi, 1986, 1991; Portes & MacLeod, 1996; Portes & Stepick, 1993; Steinberg, 1996; Waters, 1996). Proponents of this perspective propose that social capital[55] within an immigrant's family and community can strengthen and promote values of academic success for children of immigrants and may be inversely related to (or weakened by) the process of "becoming American" (Coleman, 1990;

Hagan, MacMillan, & Wheaton, 1996; Zhou & Bankston, 1996).

Second-generation Iranians both exemplified and contradicted this increasingly adopted stance on the role of culture in the education of children of immigrants. On the one hand, they saw daily that their Iranian culture in fact played a very important role in their education. Even though the very definition of an "Iranian culture" varied from one ethnic or religious group to another and from one family to another, this possession of Iranian culture essentially meant that they were not of mainstream American culture. They had another cultural marker with which to identify, one that exalted the benefits of education. This exemplified the notion that one's ethnic culture, per se, is important to their educational success.

On the other hand, second-generation Iranians challenged the view that it was essentially their ethnic culture, as opposed to the American culture, that gave them that advantage. They contradicted modern assimilation theories, because for this group of second-generation Iranians, aspects of the American culture were also instrumental in their educational experiences. For example, these second-generation Iranians considered that their appearance, friends, and daily lives often mirrored those of their American peers, that they spoke better English than Farsi, their national tongue. The following quotation from a male Jewish Iranian sums up many second generation notion of how they considered themselves American:

> I can identify with the American kids well. I was born in this country. My major language is English; my parents started speaking English in the house when I was born. I have a U.S. passport. You know, eating Roy Rogers, instead of eating *Cholo Khoresht* for dinner.

They also revered independence and freedom as American hallmarks; those were the very reasons they and their families were here. Essentially, they believed that they were American in many respects and that American culture had indeed been instrumental in allowing them to advance themselves educationally by giving them educational autonomy.

Thus, for this group, it was the combination of the two cultures -- not either/or – but rather both cultures that had forged their educational experiences.

Being Bicultural: The Hyphenated American

A bicultural orientation refers to individuals who know and understand two different cultures (Berry, 1980, 1995; LaFramboise, Hardin, Coleman, & Gerton, 1995; Mendoza & Martinez, 1981, 1989). Ogbu and Matute Bianchi (1986) consider that individuals who are bicultural "participate in two different cultures" (p. 89). This orientation also postulates that individuals can choose "the degree and manner" with "either the second culture or his or her culture of origin" (LaFramboise et al., 1995, p. 501). For example, Sodowsky and Carey (1988) found that first-generation Asian Indians preferred to think in Indian (e.g., Hindi), although they were extremely proficient in English, or that they preferred Indian food and dress at home but American food and style of dress outside their homes.

The presence of two cultures, often in harmony, other times in discord, was evident among these second-generation Iranians. For instance, their Iranian culture provided them with family support, a strong sense of roots, and the motivation to use educational opportunities. Yet that culture also restricted them, particularly when it came to socializing in the American context (e.g., difficulties with dating). They associated their sense of independence, their menu of opportunities, and their feelings of freedom with their acquisition of the American culture. And, simultaneously they rejected negative aspects of American culture: a scant sense of belonging, minimal respect for family and elderly, and not being deeply rooted historically. It was clear that they identified with certain features of each culture and decided the degree and manner to which they identified with each.

Second-generation Iranians skillfully integrated aspects of both cultures to advance themselves educationally. That is, although Iranian culture played a positive educational role among second-generation Iranians, it was in concert with aspects of the American culture that they had elected to adopt. Moreover, I propose that the combination of these two cultures may be considered a blend of structural and cultural assimilation.

Structural Versus Cultural Assimilation

Structural assimilation refers to adopting the norms and values of social institutions (Hurst, 1998). Cultural assimilation is the strategy by which individuals abandon their original cultural identity and acquire a new identity in their new environment (Berry, 1980; Laframboise, et al.). The combination of structural and cultural assimilation was illustrated in Rashid's (1984) study, in which African Americans functioned effectively and productively within America's core institutions while maintaining a sense of their African ethnic identity. Similarly, many scholars have argued that Iranian immigrants have been able to integrate themselves into the American middle class, but that their integration is structural, not cultural (Bozorgmehr & Sabagh, 1988; Chaichian, 1997; Hoffman, 1988, 1989; Naficy, 1993). That is, Iranians have taken advantage of the avenues through which they can succeed economically in the United States but have resisted assimilating into the American culture.

In terms of cultural assimilation, Iranian families bestowed a powerful sense of culture upon their second generation. Knowing that they had a rich cultural tradition to draw from grounded them more in their culture than did whether or not they maintained Farsi. Thus family closeness – caring for and spending time with family – was key to their sense of culture being preserved. Among these second-generation Iranians, the dinner table often symbolized the coming together as a family around a common cultural tradition. The concept of the dinner table was a frequently recurring theme among second-generation Iranians as a juncture between family and culture. In the realm of the family, perhaps within the symbolism of a dinner table with traditional *polo-khorest*[56], their self-esteem was nurtured, their cultural identity developed, and their educational expectations raised.

As for structural assimilation, the acquisition of English enhanced the educational opportunities of Iranian Americans. For example, they talked about performing better on standardized tests, writing better college applications, or even writing better class essays. Many commented on how, during college and/or job interviews, their command and mastery of the English language helped them gain the advantage over those who did not possess the same level of language skills. Mastering English did not connote an abandonment of their culture; rather, it gave them equal opportunities – both educationally and economically – to access the structures of American society. Thus, it was not moving away from their parents' language(s) that second-generation Iranians equated with "Americanizing." Their references to becoming American were mainly couched in the independent nature of the American society: when they ate their meals individually, for example, as opposed to eating with their family. Or, they thought Americanizing had to do with the amount of time they spent doing things: again, the dinner table became the analogy, such as when they spent time with their family around the dinner table as opposed to ordering fast-food because they had little time to be with the family. In a similar fashion, the use of English inside and outside the home was not associated with their family becoming more American. Rather, they thought that English enabled them to penetrate American institutions, thus ensuring successful membership in this society.

Language

One salient component of successful assimilation into American society for second-generation Iranians has been the acquisition and perfection of English. Rather than being forbidden or discouraged to speak English at home, they were encouraged. Mastering English meant that second-generation Iranians would improve their academic performance and further guarantee their success in higher education.

Yet language has been extensively used as the key index of cultural assimilation (Rumbaut, 1997). Gordon (1964) popularized this connection with his "straight line" hypothesis: he predicted that, over time and generation, increasing linguistic assimilation was equated with the "anglicization" of self-identity, a process that would ensure successful integration into the American society (p. 86). It is this notion that proponents of bilingual education have used as the cornerstone of their counter-argument. They contend that policies derived from this ideology "delegitimize the culture and language of parents, thus promoting dissonant acculturation.... By instilling in children the sense that their parents' language is inferior and should be quickly abandoned in favor of English, schools help drive a wedge across generations, weakening parental efforts to preserve a common cultural memory.... Self-esteem, educational expectations, and academic achievement suffer accordingly" (Portes & Rumbaut, in press, p. 7). In the context of Iranian immigrants in the United States, one can see many problems with current approaches to bilingual education. For example, how do we provide access to Farsi-speaking ESL (English as a Second Language) teachers for Iranians scattered across the United States? Iranians of Armenian, Turkish, and Kurdish ancestry are often raised with both their national language, Farsi, and their ethnic language (Armenian, Turkish, or Kurdish). How do we determine, then, which vernacular is most important among Iranians?

The Iranian example points out many of the caveats surrounding bilingual education, particularly as the argument integrates two forms of immigrant adaptation, structural and cultural. One's ethnic culture can be preserved despite the maintenance or neglect of its related language.[57] The promotion and respect of immigrants' ethnic culture encompasses a broader context of factors, including the school community, the immigrant family, and the society at large. The experiences of these second-generation Iranians reveals that it is the navigation of these broader contextual factors that challenges their immigrant ethnic identity.

To propose that these second-generation Iranians successfully integrated two cultures and that their experiences surrounding the two realms has been without confusion and frustration would not properly represent their experiences. In the next section, I present their ambivalence surrounding their combined cultural identities.

Tensions: Experiences Between Two Cultures

Though second-generation Iranians could pick and choose aspects of the two cultures that they could use to advance themselves, they did not feel fully part of either. They stressed that while they felt they had both cultures within them, they often felt confused and ambivalent as to where they fell between the two. That middle ground was often a painful experience growing up in American society. A female Muslim student who grew up in Texas recalled how growing up amidst her very "American surroundings" marked her as the outsider, as the one who did not belong, even though she was born and raised in Texas. Her experiences mirror that of many recent published personal accounts of other second-generation Iranians. Even though these accounts foretell the experiences of those who have similarly been immigrants, these second-generation Iranians felt that it was unique to them and therefore to being an Iranian-American. For example, in her poem "My

Turn," Fatemi (1999) conjures a bitter experience growing up as a second-generation Iranian:

Third grade recess
We sit in the playground
A circle of girls
One by one:
I'm one half German one
Quarter French one quarter Dutch
I'm one quarter Swiss one quarter
Belgian one half Italian one half
So many fractions I crave
Pieces of beautiful European cultures
The one we learn about in school
Details drilled into our minds
I'm one half American
One half Persian
A girl scowls
Both your parents are from
Over there
Aren't they?
I stammer *but I was born here*
She rolls her eyes
You're not half American
You are one hundred percent
I-rain-e-an
I dig chin into chest
Clench leg muscles tight
So I won't run.

But it is a recollection that has resounded throughout history, in different forms and contexts, among individuals of different backgrounds. It is, therefore, an immigrant sentiment that has been shaped by the experiences of Iranian-Americans.

Karim (1999), also writing about his experiences as a second-generation Iranian, repeats the same theme of being different: "[M]y childhood had been devoted to explaining what kind of name I had, why I ate lamb instead of hamburgers, and rice instead of potatoes. I was different" (p. 18). Their confusion about being Iranian American often surfaced in their homes when Iranian parents worried about the social interactions of their children. In that sense, Ansari (1992) found that Iranian parents are "anguished about the Americanization of their children" and constantly remind them that "you are not American, you are Iranian born in the United States" (p. 106). The frustration, confusion, and ambivalence of the two worlds of second-generation Iranians has been the source of many recent publications (see Asayesh, 1999; Bahrampour, 1999; Karim & Khorrami, 1999; Rachlin, 1995).

Mere names often crystallized the dichotomy between the cultures that shaped the experiences of second-generation Iranians. In their names, their sense of being in two cultures came to a head. Without accents and with physical appearances resembling those of Americans, they blended in. But their names singled them out, gave them away as not being part of the American mainstream. They felt frustrated having their names mispronounced, ridiculed, and questioned – "What kind of a name is that?" It was an incessant reminder that they were different, not the same, no matter how outwardly American they appeared. Their names placed them in between cultures.

Among the four ethnic-religious groups in this study, this confusion was sometimes directed not just at two cultures but at three, including the culture derived from their religion. Jewish Iranians, for instance, often felt uncertainty when they did not know what part of them was American, Iranian, or Jewish. The confusion that the participants in this study voiced reflected what Feher (1998) called the "tricultural conflict":

When you are in Iran, you are a Persian Jew. But here, you have to face the fact that you're a Persian American Jew. So you have to deal with the fact that part of your identity is coming from the Persian society and part of it from the American society. (p. 79)

Interestingly, even though second-generation Iranians described a great deal of frustration and confusion about their sense of self caught in between two (or three) cultures, they also took the difference to mean that they have unique characteristics that average Americans do not possess. For example, they had a unique name that everyone would remember or they had a lot to tell about their culture when asked where they were from. Thus, they often used the difference of their cultural background to their advantage. In some ways, they wanted to say "we're unique," to contrast themselves with those who were simply "average." Yet in other ways they wanted the same educational and economic advantages open to all Americans. In this sense, these second-generation Iranians strategically adopted aspects of American culture that would ensure them educational and economic success (structural assimilation) while disregarding features that would blend them in socially (cultural assimilation).

Socioeconomic Status

In this section, I examine the role of socioeconomic status from two viewpoints. First, I look at family socioeconomic status as a predictor of educational experiences. I examine whether and how family resources helped shape these second-generation Iranians' outlook on their education. Second, I consider socioeconomic status as a motivating factor behind their educational experiences.

Family Status

Socioeconomic status – parents' education, employment, and income -- is a major predictor of children's scholastic achievement (Brantlinger, 1993; Cazden, 1963; Coleman, 1990; Karabel & Halsey, 1977; Loury, 1987). Children

from higher socioeconomic families have advantages that
pay off in academic achievement (Lareau, 1987). Since
they generally have access to more resources than children
of poorer families, they are more likely to enter school
familiar with the English language, authority structure, and
curriculum. In addition, these children often enjoy the
benefit of the better schools and more rigorous academic
programs that exist in more affluent communities.

The 1990 Census revealed that Iranians continued to
show higher than average rates of annual income: $35,836
as compared to $28,314 for other foreign-born immigrants
and $30,176 for those born in the U.S. The 1989 Consumer
Price Index (CPI) showed that Iranian males had an
adjusted mean earnings of $39,000. Moreover, 63.4 percent
of foreign-born male Iranians in the U.S. were college
graduates, as compared to 20 percent of all Americans. Yet,
despite their relative affluence, as reflected by the U.S.
Census and CPI, the socioeconomic status of Iranians
varies widely. Many Iranians who fled at the time of the
Revolution were able to bring their wealth with them.
Those who fled during the Iran-Iraq war, when its borders
were closed to prevent migration, came with barely any
resources.[58] Some who had family connections in the
United States managed to get here with little more than the
knowledge of the abundant educational opportunities here
that their homeland did not offer them and their children.

A lot of Iranians do live in Beverly Hills and drive
the BMW's and stuff. But I wouldn't say that about
the Bahá'í community. 'Cause a lot of them
escaped. Other Iranian groups who weren't
persecuted, who didn't have trouble leaving Iran,
and who were able to make lives in Iran, like being
able to get an education things like that, were able
to bring their wealth here. But the Bahá'í
community excelled through education once they
got here so they ended up being middle class and
upper class citizens of America. But they started

from scratch. Since they were deprived in Iran they have that drive here.

Many of the participants in this study reiterated the same theme – that their families came here with barely any resources. Yet, regardless of financial wealth, all second-generation Iranians in my sample displayed a similar zeal towards their education that was transferred to them by their parents. What role, then, did social status play in the educational experience of second-generation Iranians? It was not necessarily their families' high socioeconomic status that allowed them to succeed educationally. Rather, it was their will to acquire higher socioeconomic status, or their aspirations for higher socioeconomic status, that shaped their educational experiences.

Aspirations for Socioeconomic Status

Studies of socioeconomic status have been mostly concentrated on academic outcomes rather than on achievement motivation. Yet, the desire, or the motivation to acquire higher status was a prominent feature of second-generation Iranians' educational experiences. These students wanted to achieve high socioeconomic status and their desire to pursue an education was largely shaped by this aspiration. Moreover, the tendency of socioeconomic status as a motivator was dual faceted.

These youth distinguished between two types of status– economic and symbolic– as having propelled them to advance educationally. Economic status meant acquiring wealth, while symbolic status meant acquiring educational degrees that would signal that they have earned respect and acceptance. It was their eagerness for both that propelled their educational drive. Bourdieu (1984) states that "the accumulation of economic capital merges with the accumulation of symbolic capital, that is, with the accumulation of a reputation for competence and an image of respectability and honourability that are easily converted into political positions as a local or national notable" (p. 291). Signaling has been commonly referred to in the labor market literature as the mechanism by which educational degrees are used to "signal" potential employers of one's position in the labor market (Spence, 1973). In this social realm, coupled with the particularities of this group, I believe their degrees would provide them with what I have distinguished as a "social signal of achievement" as a form of symbolic capital.

But while these second-generation Iranians admitted to striving for both economic and symbolic capital, they stressed the importance of symbolic status above and beyond its related counterpart, economic status, as the driving force behind their desires to advance educationally.

As explained earlier, a typically cited national character among Iranians has been the emphasis of social class. Pliskin (1987) explains that because the Iranian society is both hierarchical and socially mobile, social interactions are influenced by one's appearance and "one's external appearance and behavior are not necessarily indicative of one's actual condition" (p. 58). Reared in that society, first-generation Iranians are cognizant of social positions. Since social positions influence their daily lives, substantial effort is put into keeping up appearances (Bateson, 1979). I suggest that first-generation Iranians passed the importance of this characteristic onto their children, since earning professional titles continues to be prominent among this group.

The continued importance and appearance of status as a national character among this immigrant group has been discussed in a variety of newspaper and magazine articles about the wealth of the Iranian community in various U.S. cities. For example, a New York Times article[59] described the Iranian community settled in Great Neck, New York as follows:

> In the last 10 years, as Persian synagogues, restaurants and shops opened, thousands more Iranians moved in and this upscale community

became the biggest center of Iranian Jewish life on the East Coast.... They are not just moving in but moving up: Persians are responsible for much of the housing boom on the Great Neck peninsula, where palatial homes are being built on lots where ranches and Cape Cod-style cottages once stood.... Suddenly comes this group, they are impeccably groomed, they have money, they live in beautiful homes (Fischeler, 1999, p. 1).

My own observations of the Iranian community center and various Iranian events reaffirmed that establishing such status is very important among this community. When I attended a community center event casually dressed (see chapter 3), I became aware of the potential for my clothing and appearance to affect how they perceived my status. In order to blend in, I would have needed to display an outward appearance of high status.

My subjects further validated the importance of status in our interviews. Many said that their families created the illusion that they were wealthier than they really were, that in many ways their families struggled economically. After one of my interviews was "formally" over, one male Jewish-Iranian participant asked if he could talk about the issue of appearances and status among Iranians. Reluctant to talk about a negative feature of the Iranian character, he apprehensively revealed his frustration with the Iranian community:

I don't understand the need to show what you have. We are not modest people by any means. I know people who have two mortgages but have to drive a Mercedes. Why do that to yourself?

A Muslim female participant confirmed her pessimism about the role of status in the Iranian culture when she said:

In Southern California, every Mercedes around you see belongs to an Iranian person. They can live in a little shack yet go out and buy themselves a Mercedes and drive around. I don't know why *hameesheh mekhan poz bedan* (show off) to each other? What's the big deal? Like my family this and my family this! Who cares about your family, what are *you*?

Despite their criticism, it was this same phenomenon of wanting their community to know of their successes – the social signal of achievement – that motivated second-generation Iranians to advance themselves educationally. Their college majors were based on their desires to acquire social respect. These students picked areas of study – predominantly in math and the sciences – that were predicated on a belief that these types of degrees with titles would establish that they have been successful educationally. The potency of social signals of achievement through education was summarized by one Jewish-Iranian male from Great Neck:

When you want to get married and you want to get married into the Persian culture, in Great Neck, for example, families care that he is *agha doctor-é* [a doctor][60] you know, or *vakeel- é* [lawyer]. They don't care what kind of a person he is. If I wanted to marry the most beautiful girl from the best family in the world, and even though my dad's a doctor, but if I was a plumber they'd probably wouldn't let their daughter marry me as successful as some plumbers or electricians might be. I know some electricians that make more money than a doctor but an electrician is an electrician and a doctor is a doctor. I think the lawyer or a doctor is the separation.

Among Jewish Iranians, status was a theme that encompassed their newfound right of belonging in American society. They no longer had an excuse for not achieving social and economic success. In this country they were not held back by the political structures of a predominantly Islamic society. Feher (1998) found a similar conviction among the Iranian-Jewish community she studied. Her respondents explained that in the United States, Iranian Jews can no longer claim an inability to succeed because "the mullahs didn't let us" (p. 79). This sentiment that there is no excuse not to succeed also resonated among my Jewish participants. Obtaining higher degrees of education, therefore, was to establish one's higher level of status – both symbolically and economically.

Thus, the educational experiences of these young Iranians were effectively related to three factors in their lives: family, culture and their aspirations of social status. Within the family environment they were nurtured with a strong sense of heritage and a stronger sense of their educational opportunities in this country. By having the autonomy to make their own educational choices, they felt responsible for their own futures. They also sensed that they came from a rich heritage, they had roots that made them proud. As such, their parents had effectively communicated to them that education was a luxury in Iran, that they had educational opportunities here that most Iranians could only dream about. This powerful sense of where they came from and the educational opportunities that they had at their disposal was coupled with the responsibility they were given. Collectively, these forces created an educational responsibility, which was a striking feature of this immigrant group's form of discipline – a discipline model based on mutual respect.

In sum, Iranians' new generation has strategically incorporated aspects of two cultures; each has provided them with avenues to reach their educational goals without sacrificing either of their cultures.

CHAPTER SIX

Only One Piece of the Puzzle

Iranian immigrants share a common national heritage, but they are internally quite diverse – politically, religiously, ethnically, and economically. For instance, there are at least eight religious-ethnic groups among Iranians: Muslims, Jews, Armenians, Assyrians Christians, Bahá'ís, Kurds, Turks, and Zoroastrians. Iranian immigrants often identify themselves in terms of their religion and/or ethnicity and nationality (see chapter two). In this study I looked at four of these groups (Muslims, Jews, Bahá'ís, and Armenians) and found that each group brought to this country experiences, memories, and resources as varied as their religious-ethnic backgrounds. They also brought something similar: a conviction about the power and value of education.

Two points illustrated the importance of education among this sample of second-generation Iranians. One was that the fathers of this group had unusually high levels of education as compared to other immigrant groups and native-born Americans. And, two, was the fact that this sample is comprised of college students also attests to the significance of education in their lives. I strove to discover why education was so highly prized among this group? What factors led to the promotion of this institution? I discovered that three factors were salient in their educational experiences: family, culture, and a motivation to attain high socioeconomic status. In this final and concluding section, I discuss why I believe these three factors were the most important to this group. What was the relationship among family, culture, and a motivation to succeed socioeconomically? Why were not teachers and schools, for example, as important in their experiences? How could educators -- so critical in the education of youth -- be so absent in the experiences of these second-generation Iranians? Moreover, can my conclusions about this group be extended or generalized to other second-generation Iranians?

Certainly, family, culture, and a desire to acquire socioeconomic status were three interrelated links to the migration history of these second-generation Iranians. They were part and parcel of the experience of being uprooted and then transplanted: the process of moving from their homeland and resettling in a new land. The experience of migration is the unifying link among these three factors.

Uprooted: Leaving Iran Behind

The encounter of being uprooted had a powerful impact on Iranian families. The ways these second-generation Iranians described their families' influence on them was embedded in their families' migration history: they offered indelible descriptions of their families' departure from Iran. Some were born in Iran and moved here while very young, and thus had some recollection of their family's migration. Others were born here and had only heard from their parents about their exodus from Iran. Nearly all were left with a deeply felt sense that their families had abandoned their homeland. A female Bahá'í, for example, recalled how she and her family, stowed in the back of a truck of a drug dealer, traveled by night to the Pakistani border:

We had to go to one of the villages on the outskirts and pretend that we were one of the villagers and that we were visiting one of our families in the village. So we had to take a bus and go to the village. From there we had to transfer to another bus that took us to the *beyaboon* [desert]. From there we got into a pickup truck, and it had to be in the middle of the night and the lights had to be off so that no one could see us on the border. And then close to the border we split up into two different trucks. One for the women and one for the men. The men's truck got stopped by Pakistani soldiers and they had to bribe them not to send them back. And we got back together in Pakistan.

Although she was only five, her feelings of being uprooted from Iran were etched in her mind. Like her, a young Jewish woman who was born in Rhode Island and had never been to Iran felt similar and powerful feelings of having left a homeland. She wrote her college essay about her parents' flight from Iran, which had left her family with feelings of being uprooted. In these powerful renditions, one hears how family is the central influence for second-generation Iranians.

The process of migration, of being torn from their homeland, was the essence of these second-generation Iranians' ability to maintain what I have called their "point of reference." These young Iranians respected their parents' decision to leave their lives behind and appreciated the ordeal they faced at having to let go of their country. One major reason they were given for this decision was that the U.S. offered educational opportunities unavailable in Iran.

The power of education has been part of Iran's 2500-year history and is woven through the country's social fabric. Early Zoroastrian scriptures promoted education as a moral duty; Islamic principles followed similar doctrines on the value of education, though primarily for men. Throughout the country's history, Iranian monarchs have used education to maintain the status quo, and to control the social, economic, and political situation of its people. In the hierarchical social structure of Iranian society, education was the only means by which Iranians could find social mobility, acceptance, and respect. Access to education was generally limited to those within Iran's upper society. Those who had higher education credentials not only benefited financially but who, more importantly, gained social acceptance and respect. First-generation Iranians brought with them this belief that education would guarantee social status and passed it on to the next generation being reared here. The importance of education was transferred to their new lives, in a new land, to a new generation.

Transplanted: A New Life in United States

The process of being transplanted also influenced the educational experiences of second-generation Iranians. Iranians who migrated to the United States, particularly in the early 1980s, found that their self-imposed exile had placed them in a hostile host environment.[61] Until their large influx during the late 1970s and early 1980s, Iranians in the U.S. had typically been college students and/or tourists and therefore had limited social contact with the American public. Those who came as a result of the Iranian Revolution came into closer social contact with the American public as they moved into neighborhoods, entered the labor force, and sent their children to public schools.

Growing up amidst the political tension between Iran and the United States was particularly challenging for the new generation of Iranians being reared here. They came into contact with Americans in schools – a place that reflected the sentiments of the broader society. It was not until the latter part of the 1990s that several events between the two nations began to chisel away at the negative images of Iranians permeating the U.S. society. Also, Iranian-made movies were featured in mainstream U.S. cinemas.[62] As second-generation Iranians came of age in the United States, there was a thawing U.S.-Iran relationship and Iranian youth began to feel comfortable and proud to publicly discuss their experiences (see Asayesh, 1999; Bahrampour, 1999; Feher, 1998; Karim & Khorrami, 1999; Rachlin, 1995). Students in my sample talked about wearing t-shirts with "Iran" boldly written across their chests; participating in their schools' multicultural fairs as representatives of Iranian culture; and decorating their dormitory rooms with posters of Iran and/or its flag, though many had never even been to Iran. In contrast to first-generation Iranians, this younger group openly displayed their sense of pride for their heritage. A decade earlier, this sort of cultural proclamation would most likely have had a negative reception by the American public.

The Iranian culture became a marker by which they could claim an identity separate from being "the average American" as well as other immigrant groups. For these second-generation Iranians, asserting their Iranian identity meant having something to draw upon that ordinary Americans did not have, something that gave them an added advantage. They used this cultural difference to advance themselves educationally, to obtain degrees that both gave them socioeconomic status and signaled their successful achievements.

Higher education credentials served as social signals of achievement in two spheres of their lives. First, in a society that stereotyped these second-generation Iranians as uncivilized and barbaric, they proved themselves otherwise through education. They had assumed the role of "cultural diplomats" of their families' distorted and misunderstood culture, and education was the means by which they countered those negative images. If they felt hostility, they attributed the negative comments to the abusive person's ignorance rather than internalizing it. As one student told me, "I look around me, the Iranians I know are all educated … it must be the ignorance of that [other] person."

Second, in the Iranian community education also served as an equally, if not more, important social signal of achievement. Second-generation Iranians in my sample idealized the belief that educational degrees could afford them respect and acceptance, couching this desire in the notion that educational degrees were social signals of achievement. Professional titles such as a doctor or lawyer implied success. The importance that these students placed on earning respect, particularly from Iranian families and friends, was commonly voiced by my sample. For example, one Muslim woman who grew up in California told me how family friends altered their attitudes toward her once they found out she was a pre-law major:

> A lot of people in the California Iranian community where I live used to think that I was stupid because I struggled in school. I went back home for four days for Thanksgiving and went to my best friend's birthday party and they had the whole family there. Our family and friends who did not know I was in town said "we were talking about you all day today." They didn't even know I was in town, and they were asking "when are you going to become a lawyer." They seemed so interested and had this respect for me that they didn't ever have before. And it's just because I am in criminal justice! So it's really interesting how they perceive me now. I think I've made an impact on them.

The respect she had received from family and friends was clearly far more important to her than what her degree would mean to her personally (and/or financially). Even though many second-generation Iranians in my study stated their frustrations with what they saw as Iranians' desire to "show off" or to appear as high status, they were aware of this attitude among their second generation.

As part of being transplanted, this immigrant group has carried over some of their ideals about education to their new setting. Back in Iran, titles derived from higher levels of education signified social achievement and allowed for social mobility. This ideal has been brought over with them and passed on to a new generation. In a society that tended to stereotype them as "terrorists," second-generation Iranians have used educational degrees to counter social impressions. Their notion of achieving through education rested on a belief that they had *something* beneficial culturally that average Americans did not possess.

While my research illuminated what factors were relevant in the educational experiences of Iranians who grew up in the United States, it also opened up broader theoretical and practical questions. For instance, the role of schools, the institution central to one's educational experiences, was rarely mentioned in the lives of this group of second-generation Iranians. Below I address the implications I believe my research has on practice, theory, and the future of research on this topic.

Implications for Educators: Practice and Theory

This research uncovered factors that were relevant to second-generation Iranians' educational experiences and others that were not, including the role of professors, teachers and counselors, and schools in general. Why were they not central to this group of students' experiences? Perhaps these immigrants implicitly assumed that they had the resources and skills that would ensure them entry into and success in American society. Perhaps teachers felt that precious time and attention should not be devoted to a group that seemed to already value education. Maybe the second-generation Iranians wanted to "blend in" within this institution to guarantee themselves equal opportunities, and so did not want educators to single them out as requiring special services. Whatever the reason, second-generation Iranians whom I studied clearly did not consider their current professors or past teachers and/or counselors to be an important part of their educational experiences. This lack of importance of educators in their experiences has profound implications.

Had this group not had the family support network that they did and/or pride in their heritage, the school could have become a devastating arena. In some of their narratives, I found that teachers – sometimes knowingly and other times unintentionally –promoted the negative stereotypes these students were already facing in the broader society. The lack of connection between educators and these youth also brings to the fore some of the recent arguments made about the "model minority myth" (Ima, 1995). Assuming that certain children will do well because of their backgrounds, as in the case with Asians, can ultimately have negative repercussions as educators miss children who are likely to fall through the cracks. In terms of its implications for practice, this study reaffirms the importance of recognizing and understanding diversity among America's students.

In terms of theory, the issue of language among second-generation Iranians demonstrated that promoting English does not necessarily equate with the obliteration of an immigrant group's original or ethnic culture. Proponents of bilingual education argue that promoting English over the immigrant group's original language is detrimental to their cultural identity (Portes, 2000). Yet, as I discovered from this group of students, mastering English – or, inversely, abandoning Farsi was not necessarily associated with abandonment of their heritage or culture. For this group, culture was multifaceted and nurtured in a variety of contexts; language was not the only cultural marker.

The issue of language and cultural identity need to be further explored in future studies. For instance, I wonder if the parents of these students held similar convictions about the nature of language and cultural identification as did their children. Moreover, how would the parents respond to their children's perception of not being pressured educationally? Are they laissez-faire because this group did well academically and what would have been their response had they not performed well. Although many of my participants remarked that their parents did not pressure them even when their grades were low, I wonder what the parental consensus would be on that front. The responses that these students shared, juxtaposed to that of their parents, would provide us with more insightful conclusions. For both theory and practice, this study points to the importance of a transnational understanding of immigrants. We must understand the context that immigrants come from just as much as we try to understand how they are integrating in the United States.

Implications for Future Research

This study raised two methodological issues: data collection and sampling criteria.

Data Collection

As I mentioned in chapter three, there are limitations to interviews. They take place at a constrained place and time, during which the interviewees reveal limited features of their lives; the interviewer captures an even more limited picture of their experiences. In retrospect, I recognize that a longitudinal study would have yielded results that would have enabled me to validate my findings by seeing if their narratives maintained the same story line over time. Perhaps some comments would then have been dismissed as temporal, rather than as reflecting long-held beliefs or ideas. In a longer study, I would have also arranged to meet with these students in a variety of contexts – in their homes and schools, and on social occasions such as outings with peers or Iranian gatherings.

Sampling

One sampling criterion in this study was that students had to have Iranian-born parents. Yet part of the migration experience is inter-marriage – Iranians marrying Americans or other nationalities. As I found throughout the course of this study when trying to find participants, many second-generation Iranians have both Iranian and American parents. Though I did not formally interview children of such mixed marriages, I think their insights into the experience of "second-generation" Iranians would be intriguing. Many talked about how the cultural schism I saw between the family and the public lives of second-generation Iranians played out within their homes. In some respects, they, too, held on to their Iranian culture as a way of distinguishing themselves from "average" Americans, or of being unique. Further studies should bring forth the voices, histories, and experiences of second-generation Iranians growing up in the middle of a "cultural hyphen."

Finally, as I've mentioned throughout this study, Iranians are diverse in terms of religion and ethnicity. Their migration to this country has made them even more diverse in terms of where they have settled, mostly the East or West Coast. I found some evidence to suggest that the experiences of second-generation Iranians on the East Coast are different from those on the West Coast. Southern California, for instance, is dubbed Irangeles, and is home to an Iranian-American pop culture (see Naficy, 1993). The concentration of Iranians, with their shop-lined streets, has created the illusion of an Iran in exile. It is plausible that the experiences of second-generation Iranians growing up near or in an Iranian community differs from those who grew up without a physical community.

In conclusion, this study captured only one glimpse into the educational experiences of Iranians' new generation who grew up in the United States, adding a puzzle piece to our knowledge of immigrants who have moved to this country.

Notes

[1] The Safavid Dynasty (1502-1736) was an Iranian dynasty that established Shi'ite Islam as its state religion. This became a major factor in the emergence of a unified national consciousness among the various ethnic and linguistic elements of the country.

[2] The Iranian Revolution is also referred to as the Islamic Revolution.

[3] Islamic Republic of Iran Census Data (1986) reported an annual growth rate estimated at 4 percent. Since then, they claim that they have been able to limit the growth to 2.8 percent (Christian Science Monitor, April 28, 1995).

[4] For a good discussion of these religious, ethnic, and linguistic differences, see Richard F. Nyrop's (1978) Iran: A Country Study (pp. 139-154).

[5] Iran's census data does not collect religious and/or ethnicity data. The following figures have been extensively quoted in the literature (Halliday, 1979; Simpson & Shubart, 1995; Wilber, 1981).

[6] The Pahlavi reign began in 1920 with Reza Shah and ended in 1979 when his son Mohammed Reza Shah was overthrown by the Islamic revolutionaries. Throughout their time in power, both Pahlavis pushed to modernize Iran and make it into a major world power. The institution that they believed gave them the means to achieve their goal was education. They also believed that religion (Islam) would hinder their development plans and therefore censored Islamic values from textbooks and virtually abolished all forms of *maktabs* (religious schools) (Mohsendour, 1988).

[7] SAVAK is an acronym for Sazemane Ettela'at Va-Amniyate Keshvar, Iran's state intelligence and security organization.

[8] Hosain was a religious martyr. The event of his martyrdom has been a day of great mourning among Shi'i Moslems. The day is the tenth day (*Ashura*) of the first month (*Moharam*) of the Muslim year. Keddie (1981) refers to the martyrdom of Hosain during periods of political discontent as a "paradigm of just struggle again unrighteous tyrants, a theme often given explicit political resonance" (p. 184).

[9] Khomeini continued his propaganda and was finally exiled in 1964.

[10] Bill (1972) defines higher education as any postsecondary training or study, including the teachers training colleges, polytechnic institutes, and educational centers associated with the ministries that offered compact training programs initiated to meet new tasks.

[11] The creation of the literacy corps (article 6) and free schooling at all levels of education (article 15) were two of the nineteen articles of the Shah's White Revolution (*Enqelab-e Sefeed*). The White Revolution was a monumental mission by the Shah through which he intended to create a just society. It was also the mechanism by which he wanted to drive Iran toward the "most advanced countries of the world." At the center of his reform agenda was land reform legislation. Three of his articles dealt with education. Other principles included nationalization of forests and water resources, administrative reform, the transformation of industrial workers into shareholders, electoral reform, the creation of "health corps" and "reconstruction corps," antiprofiteering and anticorruption campaigns, and social insurance (Pahlavi, 1961).

[12] Beginning in early 1962, the government legislated and implemented the first of several phases of its land reform policies. While the original intent of the regime was to transfer land ownership from large landowners to peasants, poorly constructed and implemented land reform policies did little for the majority of Iran's peasants in terms of getting land. The unplanned consequence of land reform policies during this time period caused a large migration to cities of both laborers and poor peasants.

[13] Of this group only seven percent were women (Wilber, 1981).

[14] Non-Islamic youths from Armenian, Jewish, or Zoroastrian backgrounds were reported to cope more effectively.

[15] One of the strongest opposition groups, with leftist influences, was known as the Confederation of Iranian Students. Other groups included Muslim students' associations. Many of the leaders of the Revolution

(including Abolhassan Bani Sadr, Ibrahim Yazdi, and Sadq Ghotbzadeh) were members of student organizations abroad.

[16] This provision did not include those of the Baha'i faith.

[17] The Carter administration allowed the deposed Shah to enter the United States to seek medical treatment for his lymphoma cancer, citing it as "medical humanitarianism" (Altman, 1979). The act was seen by Iranians as a "symbolic insult" (Fischer, 1980). Khomeini used the act to mobilize the Iranian public towards creating his ideal Islamic society, free of Western influences. On Students' Day, the day that honored the slayings of students at Tehran University, several hundred students seized the United States Embassy. They took sixty-three hostages and demanded that the Shah be returned to Iran to stand trial. The support of such an act by those living abroad, particularly in the United States, was subdued. Only a handful of students chained themselves to the Statue of Liberty in New York to show their protest.

[18] In 1980, the number of Iranian students in the U.S. was 51,310. In 1984 this figure declined to 20,260. The decline has been attributed to the political tensions between the U.S. and Iran, financial constraints, and inability to leave Iran due to the war.

[19] The horrific Iran-Iraq war lasted eight years. The war cost Iran an estimated $600 billion. There was an approximate $450 billion worth of infrastructure/property damage; 400,000-700,000 people injured; and 160,000 deaths. There are estimates that between 400,000 to 700,000 Iranians were maimed in the war; the regime has committed to paying benefits to disabled veterans, widows, and orphans. Throughout the eight-year war, half of Iran's GNP was consumed by the war efforts (Hipo, 1993; Hooglund, 1989).

[20] The changes were at all educational levels.

[21] Either their classrooms were divided by curtains, or men were required to sit in the back, women in the front.

[22] Fatwa is an Islamic verdict.

[23] Several people were murdered during the violent campaign to kill Salman Rushdie and others connected to the publishing of the book. They include Hitoshi Igarashia, the Japanese translator of the book, who was murdered; the Italian translator was beaten and stabbed; the Norwegian publisher was shot.

[24] Initially after the Iran-Iraq war, men's compulsory military service could be purchased at a rate of $10,000. More recently, the rates have been as low as $750 (Phone interview, Interests Section of the Islamic

Republic   of   Iran,   Washington,   D.C.).   Also   available: http://www.daftar.org/

[25] In Farsi, *Azad* means "freedom."

[26] In 1980, President Carter signed into law the Refugee Act of 1980. This law changed the granting of asylum to only escapees from communist-controlled nations by redefining a refugee to be anyone who has a well-founded fear of persecution or physical harm, regardless of the political ideology of their home country. Despite this change in immigration policy, the majority of those granted refugee status continue to be from Communist or former communist countries (INS, 1993, table 35). Being afforded refugee status provides legal status to immigrants to work and obtain welfare benefits.

[27] It is purported that Turkey harbors the largest Iranian community outside of Iran, but there are no reliable national statistics against which I can make viable comparisons.

[28] Bozorgmehr (1998) maintains that although the Census data is relatively accurate, it does not account for "persons of Iranian origin, born in the U.S. or elsewhere, who report a different ancestry than Iranian as one of the first two ancestries that are coded (the other being American). Some persons of Iranian origin, e.g., American-born Armenians and Assyrians, are not counted if they choose one of these ancestries over Iranian" (p. 9). Bozorgmehr recognizes, however, that there is not a large enough second generation for these religious ethnicities to create a "substantial underestimation" of Iranians; nor is there a huge undocumented (illegal) Iranian population to account for variation between community claims and the U.S census data.

[29] The Harvard Encyclopedia of American Ethnic Groups reports that the number of Iranians in the United States between 1842-1930 totaled 130, increasing to 780 between 1925 and 1932. There is no record of Iranian migration between 1904-1924 and 1933-1944. Thus, only 910 Iranians are reported to have migrated to the U.S. in over a century (1842-1944). It should be noted, however, that the origins of these figures are unknown. Data reported by the Immigration and Naturalization Service for 1949 totaled 195 Iranians (Lorentz & Wertime, 1980).

[30] Visitors and students are considered non-immigrants.

[31] Defined here as those who were born in Iran or are of Iranian ancestry.

[32] Like the first wave of Cuban refugees who were typically characterized as "those who wait," this group of Iranian emigrants

came to the United States to weather the political instability of their country (Mackey & Beebe, 1969; Pedraza, 1996).

[33] For example, the Persian Watch Cat has petitioned the "cancellation of finger printing, excessive security checks of persons of Iranian heritage, a relaxation of visas for the relatives of Iranian Americans in particular, and a comprehensive survey to assess the quality of air travel and airline services taken by people of Iranian heritage, especially to Iran (see www.antidiscrimination.org).

[34] Portes (1996) defines "second generation," or children of immigrants, as children who migrated at an early age (1.5 generation) or U.S.-born children of immigrant parents.

[35] The community of Iranians in Los Angeles is referred to as Irangeles (Kelley, 1993). Of the U.S. Iranian population, 76,000 (29 percent) live in the Los Angeles region (Bozorgmehr, Der-Martirosian, and Sabagh 1996).

[36] Suárez-Orozco (2000) defines structural assimilation as "social relations and participation in the opportunity structure" and cultural assimilation, or rather, "acculturation" "in terms of language, values, and cultural identifications" (p. 8).

[37] The Iranian Yellow Page Directory is available in such areas as Washington D.C., New York, and Los Angeles. It illustrates this immigrant community's attempt to establish an ethnic economic enclave.

[38] Iranian immigrants often identify themselves in terms of both their religion and ethnicity, as well as their nationality (Bozorgmehr, Sabagh, & Der-Martirosian, 1993).

[39] Note that Baha'is and Muslims are religious groups, whereas Armenians and Jews are both religious and ethnic groups.

[40] The majority of Iranians are Shiite Muslims as opposed to Sunni Muslims who constitute approximately eight percent of the Iranian population. A majority of Kurds, virtually all Baluchis and Turkomans, and a minority of Arabs are Sunnis, as are small communities of Persians in southern Iran and Khorasan.

[41] The Second Book of Kings 17:6 actually traces Jewish settlement in Iran to the eighth century B.C. "In the ninth year of Hoshea, the king of Assyria took Samaria, and carried Israel away unto Assyria, and placed them in Halah, and in Harbor, on the river of Gozan, and in the cities of the Medes." Medea is a region in northwest Iran; its capital Ecbatana is now called Hamadan.

[42] There are approximately 125,000 Zoroastrians worldwide: 80,000 in India, 30,000 in Iran, and 3,000 in the United States (Kelley, 1993).

[43] Zoroastrians from India, called Parsis, believe that the religion is exclusively hereditary. Despite the threat of continual shrinkage in their community, they believe that it is a birthright: to be a Zoroastrian one must be born into the religion.

[44] For a critique of these and other Western perspectives on the Iranian national character, see Banuazizi (1977) "Iranian 'National Character': A Critique of Some Western Perspectives" in Psychological Dimensions of Near Eastern Studies, edited by L. Carl Brown and Norman Itzkowitz. New Jersey: The Darwin Press.

[45] This profile reflects some of the current educational and occupational statistics on Iranians in the United States. For example, the concentration of the largest Iranian community in the Los Angeles region shows that foreign-born Iranians between the ages of 25 and 64 have a wide gender gap in terms of education: 64.9 percent of men have four years of college or more as compared to only 33.7 percent of women. And in terms of occupation, the same group reveals that men have a mean income of $34,107 while women are at nearly half that, $17,441 (Bozorgmehr et al., 1996).

[46] In this sample, 86 percent of second-generation Iranians attended public schools. This compares to the U.S. average of public school enrollment of 89 percent.

[47] Ostensibly, I found that the earlier the date of migration, the greater the familiarity of the family with the U.S. educational system.

[48] I note, however, that Mashadi Jews are not entirely representative of the Iranian Jewish community.

[49] Defining the term "culture" has been the basis of much controversy, as I will discuss in the next chapter. In this context, I conceptualize culture as "the totality of equivalent and complementary learned meanings maintained by a human population, or by identifiable segments of a population, and transmitted from one generation to the next" (Rohner, 1984, p.120).

[50] Many Iranian Jews, however, do celebrate Noruz (Meleis, Lipson, & Dallalar, 1997, Dallalfar, 1999).

[51] Nyrop (1978) explains the difficulty that exists in reading and/or writing Farsi. He explains that in Farsi, "special signs written above or below the line are used to denote short vowels. These signs are only in dictionaries and textbook, which means that a reader must have substantial vocabulary to understand a newspaper, an average book, or

handwriting" (p. 141). This explains why this participant, whose Farsi was limited, found it difficult to translate the name to Farsi.

[52] *Not Without My Daughter* was a 1991 Hollywood movie about an American who marries an Iranian and they go back to Iran for a visit with their daughter. To the woman's horror, her husband decides to stay. If she wants to leave Iran, she must leave her daughter behind. If she stays, she must live in a culture vastly different, and according to the movie, very dangerous. The movie took advantage of Americans' perceptions of Iran after the unrest of the '70s and early '80s by depicting Iranians and their culture as barbaric.

[53] *Megillah* is a community magazine published by the Mashadi Youth Committee.

[54] In the early 1900s, 86 percent of the immigrants came from Europe, while only 2 percent of the immigrants came from Asia, Africa, Oceania, or Latin America. In 1990, the figures were nearly inverse with only 22 percent of the immigrant population emanating from European countries while 70 percent came from the other four continents; 67 percent of which were Asians and Latin Americans. See Appendix A.

[55] "Social capital," as differentiated from "financial" or "human capital," refers to relations between actors that "inhere in family relations and in community organization and that are useful for the cognitive or social development of a child or young person" (Coleman, 1990, p. 300). Essentially, one derives social capital from socially structured relations between individuals (e.g., parents, teachers, neighbors, and children) in social groups (e.g., families, schools, and neighborhoods) that ultimately strengthen the learning capabilities of children (Coleman, 1990).

[56] When I asked students what they typically ate at their dinner table, it was predominately *polo-khorest* (rice and an accompanying dish). When they wanted to give examples of how American their family has become, for instance, they would make references to ordering out for pizza, Chinese, or other fast-food dishes.

[57] Second-generation Iranians in this study all spoke and understood Farsi to varying degrees. Many had attended Farsi schools (particularly Muslim Iranians) when they were younger and/or had taken college courses to learn Farsi. Very few of these students claimed that they could read or write; thus Farsi was maintained in its oral form. Armenian Iranians in this sample were the least proficient in either oral or written forms of Farsi.

[58] The socioeconomic status of most Iranians changed for the worse after the Islamic Republic installed itself as Iran's new government. Many of those who had well-paying jobs lost their positions under the new form of government (e.g., professors, government officials). One of my participant's father was a filmmaker; the new Islamic government, with its tight restrictions on entertainment, banned the entertainment industry leaving her father without employment. Baha'i Iranians were not allowed to work, and if they had pensions with the former government, those were seized. The major impetus for those Iranians who fled Iran during the ensuing years was that they saw their futures in Iran as limited or hopeless. In its first five years, the period of the greatest number of Iranian immigrants to flee to the United States, Khomeini's revolutionary regime confronted a series of crises that included a 14-month confrontation with the United States over the hostage crisis; a Western arms embargo; economic isolation from most of the developed world; a near total collapse of the economy; full-scale war with Iraq; armed revolts by Kurdish and Baluchi minorities seeking autonomy; severe disaffection within the middle class and the educated elite; a serious brain drain; and a violent internal opposition (including a wave of assassinations during a period in 1981 when the Marxist Mujahedeen turned against the Ayatollah, decimating the mullah leadership) (Smith, 1984).

[59] This article was perceived by the Iranian Jewish community as derogatory as evinced by the editorials from the Iranian-Jewish community.

[60] The term "agha" literally means sir; added to the title of doctor it adds an added level of respect.

[61] On November 4, 1979, Iranian extremists took U.S. diplomats hostage and held them for 444 days. During this ordeal, anti-Iranian sentiment grew in American society. The stereotypical images of Iranians throughout the United States were of American flag-burning zealots and terrorists, violent and uncivilized (Bozorgmehr, Der-Martirosian, & Sabagh, 1993).

[62] *The White Balloon, Children of Heaven, Color of Paradise*, and *A Time for Drunken Horses* have been four Iranian movies that have been featured in American cinemas. *The White Balloon*, for example, won two awards at the 1995 Cannes Film Festival and was praised by critics worldwide. Recognizing its mass appeal, the film was distributed in major U.S. cities in the winter of 1996.

References

Afrasiabi, K. L. (1994). *After Khomeini: New Directions in Iran's Foreign Policy*. Boulder, Colorado: Westview Press.

Afshar, Haleh (Ed.) (1985). *Iran, a revolution in turmoil*. Albany: State University of New York Press.

Alba, R., & Nee, V. (1997). Rethinking assimilation theory for a new era of immigration. *International Migration Review, 31*(4), 826-874.

Altman, Lawrence K. (1979, October 25). Information Bank Abstracts. *The New York Times*.

Anderson, K. and Jack, D. C. (1991). Learning to listen: Interview techniques and analyses. In S. B. Gluck & D. Patai (Eds.), *Women's words: The feminist practice of oral history* (pp. 11-26). New York: Routledge.

Andoni, Lamis (1995, April 28). Soaps, Rock, and Democracy Dished to Iranians. *Christian Science Monitor*, p. 1.

Ansari, Abdoulmaboud (1977). A Community in Process: The First Generation of the Iranian Professional Middle-Class Immigrants in the United States. *International Review of Modern Sociology 7*: 85-101.

Ansari, M. (1992). *The making of the Iranian community in America*. New York: Pardis Press, Inc.

Ansari, M. (1997). Statistical picture of Iranian-Americans. *The Center for Iranian Research and Analysis, 13*(2), 37-39.

171

Arasteh, A. Reza (1969). *Education and social awakening in Iran, 1850-1968* (2nd ed.). Leiden, The Netherlands: E. J. Brill.

Arjomand, Said (1988). *The turban for the crown.* New York: Oxford University Press.

Asayesh, Gelareh (1999). *Saffron skies: A life between Iran and America.* Boston, MA: Beacon Press.

Askari, Hossein and Cummings, John T., and Izbudak, Mehmet (1977). Iran's migration of skilled labor to the United States. *Iranian Studies 10*(1-2), 3-35.

Bahrampour, Tara (1999). *To see and see again: A life in Iran and America.* New York: Farrar Straus & Giroux.

Bakhash, Shaul (1986). *Reign of the Ayatollahs.* New York: Basic Books.

Ballantine, Jeanne H. (1985). *Schools and society, A reader in education and sociology.* Palo Alto: Mayfield Publishing Company.

Banuazizi, Ali (1977). Iranian 'National Character': A Critique of Some Western Perspectives. In L. Carl Brown & Norman Itzkowitz (Eds.), *Psychological Dimensions of Near Eastern Studies* (pp. 210-239). New Jersey: The Darwin Press.

Bateson, Mary Catherine (1979). 'This Figure of Tinsel': A Study of Themes of Hypocrisy and Pessimism in Iranian Culture. *Daedalus 108*(3), 125-34.

Bateson, Mary Catherine (2000). *Full Circles Overlapping Lives.* New York: Random House.

Beeman, William O. (1976a). What is (IRANIAN) National Character? A Sociolinguistic Approach. *Iranian Studies 9*: 22-48.

———. (1976b). Status, Style and Strategy in Iranian Interaction. *Anthropological Linguistics 18*: 305-322.

———. (1977). The Hows and Whys of Persian Style: A Pragmatic Approach. In R. Fasold & R. Shuy (Eds.), *Studies in language variation: sematics, syntax, phonology, pragmantics, social situations, ethnographic approaches* (pp.260-282). Washington, D.C.: Georgetown University Press.

Beck, B. (1970). Cooking welfare stew. In R. Habenstein (Ed.), *Pathways to data.* Chicago: Aldine.

Behdad, Sohrab (1995). Islamization of economics in Iranian universities. *International Journal of Middle East Studies, 27*: 193-217.

Behdad, Sohrab & Saeed Rahnema (Eds.) (1995). *Iran after the Revolution: Crisis of an Islamic state*. New York: St. Martin's Press.

Benne, Kenneth (1970). Authority in education. *Harvard Educational Review, 40*(3), 385-410.

Bennett, William J. (1988). Moral literary and the formation of character. *NASSP Bulletin 72*(512), 29-34.

Benninga, Jacques S. (February 1988). An emerging synthesis in moral education. *Phi Delta Kappan 69*(6), 415-418.

Berry, J. W. (1980). Social and cultural change. In H. C. Triandis & R. Brislin (Eds.), *Handbook of cross-cultural psychology: Vol. 5. Social Psychology*. Boston: Allyn and Bacon.

Berry, J. W. (1995). Psychology of acculturation. In Nancy Rule Goldberger & Jody Bennet Veroof (Eds.), *The culture and psychology reader*. New York: New York University Press.

Bhabha, Homi K. (1994). *The location of culture*. New York: Routledge.

Bharier, Julian (1971). *Economic development in Iran 1900-1970*. New York: Oxford University Press.

Bill, James Alban (1972). *The politics of Iran: Groups, classes, and modernization*. Columbus , OH: Charles E. Merrill Publishing Company.

Binder, L. (1963). *Iran*. California: University of California Press.

Bourdieu, Pierre (1984). *Distinction: A social critique of the judgment of taste*. Cambridge, Massachusetts: Harvard University Press.

Boyer, Edward (2000, January 17). U.S.-Iranian Game is victory for harmony; soccer: Americans on both sides say the contest should inspire healing of the two nations' rift. *Los Angeles Times*, Part B, p. 1.

Bozorgmehr, M., & Sabagh, G. (1988). High status immigrants: A statistical profile of Iranians in the United States. *Iranian Studies, 21*(3), 5-35.

Bozorgmehr, M., Sabagh, G., & Der-Martirosian, C. (1993). Beyond nationality: Religious-ethnic diversity. R. Kelley, J. Friedlander, & A. Colby (Eds.), *Irangeles* (pp. 59-79). Los Angeles: University of California Press.

Bozorgmher, Mehdi (1995). Diaspora in the postrevolutionary period. *Encyclopedia Iranic, 7*: 380-383.

Bozorgmehr, M., Der-Martirosian C, & Sabagh, G. (1996). Middle Easterners: A new kind of immigrant. In R. Waldinger & M. Bozorgmehr (Eds.), *Ethnic Los Angeles* (pp. 345-378). New York: Russell Sage Foundation.

Bozorgmehr, M., & Sabagh, G. (1998). From Iranian studies to studies of Iranians in the United States. *Iranian Studies, 31*(1): 5-30.

Bozorgmehr, M. (2000). Does host hostility create ethnic solidarity? The experience of Iranians in the United States. *Bulletin of the Royal Institute for Inter-Faith Studies 2*(1), 159-178.

Brantlinger, E. A. (1993). *The politics of social class in secondary school: Views of affluent and impoverished youth.* New York: Teachers College Press.

Came, Barry (1978, November 20). Yankee go home. *Newsweek.*

Caplan, N., Whitmore, J. K., & Choy, M. H. (1989). *The boat people and achievement in America: A study of family life, hard Work, and cultural values.* Ann Arbor: University of Michigan Press.

Cazden, C. B. (1963). *Social class differences and child language: The status of our knowledge and status for further research.* Cambridge: Harvard University Press.

Chaichian, Mohammad A. (1997). First generation Iranian immigrants and the question of cultural identity: The Case of Iowa. *International Migration Review. 31*(3), 612-627.

Coleman, J. S. (1990). *Foundations of social theory.* Cambridge, MA: Belknap Press of Harvard University Press.

————. (1990). *Equality and achievement in education.* Boulder, CO: Westview Press.

Coles, Robert and Louis Genevie (1990). Is the moral fabric of our children unraveling? *Teacher,* 42-29.

Coleman, James S. (1965). *Education and political development.* Princeton, NJ: Princeton University Press.

Coombs, Philip H. (1985). *The world crisis in education.* New York: Oxford University Press.

Dallalfar, Arlene (1999). Iranian Jewish Diaspora women: Experiencing Mizrahi identity in exile. In *Studying Jewish Women: An Interchange of Ideas from 11 Countries.* Working Papers Series: International Research Institute on Jewish Women, Brandeis University.

Dallalfar, Arlene (1996). Iranian immigrant women as entrepreneurs in Los Angeles. In Barbara C. Aswad and Barbara Bilge (Eds.),

Family and gender among American Muslims: Issues facing Middle Eastern immigrant and their descendants (pp. 107-128). Philadelphia: Temple University Press.

Dalton, M. (1959). *Men who manage.* New York: John Wiley.

Durkheim, Emile (1961). *Moral education: A study in the theory and application of the sociology of education.* New York: Free Press of Glencoe.

Eisner, E. (1991). *The enlightened eye: Qualitative inquiry and the enhancement of educational practice.* New York: Macmillan.

Ekstrom, R. B., Goertz, M. E., Pollack, J. M., & Rock, D. A. (1986). Who drops out of high school and why? Findings from a national study. *Teachers College Record, 87*: 356-373.

Entessar, Nader (1984). Educational reforms in Iran: Cultural revolution or anti-intellectualism?" *Journal of South Asian and Middle Eastern Studies, 8*: 47-64.

Etessami, Mehran (2000). What we did to Great Neck ... and what Great Neck did to us. *Megillah* (67): 1.

Fatemi, Tara (1999). My turn. In P. Karim and M. M. Khorrami (Eds.) *A world between: Poems, Short Stories, and Essays by Iranian-Americans* (p. 46). New York: George Braziller.

Fattahipour, Fard (1963). Educational diffusion and the modernization of an ancient civilization. Unpublished Ph.D. dissertation, University of Chicago.

Feher, Shoshanah (1998). From the rivers of Babylon to the valleys of Los Angeles: The exodus and adaptation of Iranian Jews. In R. Stephen Warner & Judith G. Wittner (Eds.), *Gatherings in Diaspora* (pp. 71-94). Philadelphia: Temple University Press.

Fereshteh, Mohammad Hossein (1987). Modern bilateral higher education relations between Iran and the United States: 1960-1987. Unpublished Ph.D. dissertation, University of Connecticut.

Fischeler, Marcelles S. (1999, December 5). Circling the welcome wagons. *The New York Times,* Section 14LI, p. 1.

Fischer, Michael M. J. (1980). *Iran from religious dispute to revolution.* Cambridge, Massachusetts: Harvard University Press.

Foner, N. (1997). The immigrant family: Cultural legacies and cultural changes. *International Migration Review, 31*: 961-974.

Gans, H. J. (1992). Second-generation decline: Scenarios for the economic and ethnic futures of the post-1965 American immigrants. *Ethnic and Racial Studies, 15*: 173-192.

Geertz, Clifford (1973). *The interpretation of cultures.* New York: Basic Books.

Ghaffarian, Shireen (1987). The acculturation of Iranians in the United States. *The Journal of Social Psychology, 127*(6), 565-571.

Ghods, M. Reza (1989). *Iran in the Twentieth Century: A political history.* Boulder: Lynne Rienner Publishers.

Gibson, M. A. (1988). *Accomodation without assimilation: Sikh immigrants in an American high school.* Ithaca, NY: Cornell University Press.

Gilanshah, F. (1990). The formation of Iranian community in the Twin Cities from 1983-1989. *Wisconsin Sociologist, 27*(4), 11-17.

Gilligan, Carol (1982). *In a different voice.* Cambridge, MA: Harvard University Press.

Glazer, Nathan (1954). Ethnic Groups in America: From National Culture to Ideology. In Morroe Berger et al. (Eds.), *Freedom and Control in Modern Society.* New York: D. Van Nostrand and Co.

Glazer, N. (1955). The social characteristics of American Jews. *American Jewish yearbook 56*: 3-42. Philadelphia, PA: American Jewish Committee.

Goodwin, Jeff and Skocpol, Theda (1989). Explaining revolutions in the contemporary Third World. *Politics & Society, 17*(4), 489-509.

Gordon, M. M. (1964). *Assimilation in American life: The role of race, religion, and national origins.* New York: Oxford University.

Gow, Haven Bradford (1989). The true purpose of education. *Phi Delta Kappan 70*(7), 545-546.

Graham, Robert (1978). *Iran: The illusion of power.* New York: St. Martin's Press.

Haas, William (1946). *Iran.* New York: Columbia University Press.

Haddad, Yvonne Y. & Jane I. Smith (Eds.) (1994). *Muslim communities in North America.* New York: State University Press.

Hagan, John, Ross MacMillan and Blair Wheaton (1996). New kid in town: Social capital and the life course effects of family migration on children. *American Sociological Review. 61*: 368-385.

Hale, Sondra (1991). Feminist method, process, and self-criticism: Interviewing Sudanese women. In S. B. Gluck & D. Patai (Eds.),

Women's words: The feminist practice of oral history (pp. 121-36).
New York: Routledge.

Halliday, Fred (1979). *Iran: Dictatorship and development* (2nd ed.).
Penguin Books.

Herkovits, M. (1948). *Man and his works.* New York: Knopf

Hermansen, M. K. (1994). Muslims of San Diego. In Yvonne Yazbeck
Haddad & Jane Idleman Smith (Eds.), *Muslim communities in
North America* (pp.169-194). New York: State University of New
York Press.

Hernandez, D. (1993). *American's children: Resources from family,
government and the economy.* New York: Russell Sage
Foundation.

Hipo, Dilip (1993). The Iran-Iraq war. In Hooshang Amirahmadi and
Nader Entessar (Eds.), *Iran and the Arab world.* Basingstoke,
England: Macmillan.

Hoffman, D. M. (1988). Cross-cultural adaptation and learning:
Iranians and Americans at school. In H. T. Trueba & C. Delgado-
Gaitan (Eds.), *School and society: Learning content through
culture* (pp. 163-180). New York: Praeger.

Hooglund, Eric (1989). The Islamic Republic at War and Peace. *Middle
East Report*, 4-12.

Hurst, Michael (1998). *The assimilation of immigrant in the U.S. Labor
Market: Employment and labor force turnover.* New York:
Garland.

Huyser, Robert E. (1986). *Mission to Tehran.* New York: Harper &
Row.

Ima, K. (1995). Testing the American dream: Case studies of at-risk
Southeast Asian refugee students in secondary schools. In R. G.
Rumbaut & W. A. Cornelius (Eds.), *California's immigrant
children: Theory, research, and implications for educational
policy* (pp. 191-208). San Diego: University of California, Center
for U.S.-Mexican Studies.

Iranian Christian International (1996). Persian Diaspora Census 1996
[on-line data]. Available:
http://www.farsinet.com/pwo/daispora.html.

Iran Almanac and Book of Facts, 1971. (10th ed.) Tehran: The Echo of
Iran 1971.

Iran Almanac and Book of Facts, 1976. (15th ed.) *Tehran: The Echo of Iran.*

Jahoda, G. (1984). Do we need a concept of culture? *Journal of Cross-cultural Psychology, 15*: 139-151.

James, Bill (1972). The politics of Iran: Groups, classes and modernization. Columbus: Merrill.

Kahn, A. & Cannell, C. (1957). *The dynamics of interviewing.* New York: John Wiley.

Kamalkhani, Zahra (1988). *Iranian immigrants and refugees in Norway.* Bergen, Norway: University of Bergen.

Kao, G., & Tienda, M. (1995). Optimism and achievement: The educational performance of immigrant youth. *Social Science Quarterly, 76*(1), 1-19.

Karabel, J., & Halsey, A. H. (Eds.) (1977). *Power and ideology in education.* New York: Oxford University Press.

Karim, Persis M. and Mohammad Mehdi Khorrami, Eds. (1999). *A world between: Poems, short stories, and essays by Iranian-Americans.* New York: George Braziller.

Keddie, Nikki (1981). *The roots of revolution: An interpretive history of modern Iran.* New Haven: Yale University Press.

Kelley, R. (1993). Ethnic and religious communities from Iran in Los Angeles. In R. Kelley, J. Friedlander, & A. Colby (Eds.), *Irangeles* (pp. 81-161). Los Angeles: University of California Press.

―――. (1994). Muslims in Los Angeles. In Yvonne Yazbeck Haddad & Jane Idleman Smith (Eds.), *Muslim communities in North America* (pp.135-167). New York: State University of New York Press.

Khalili, Laleh (1998). Mixing memory and desire. The Iranian [on-line journal]. Available: www.Iranian.come/features/May98/Iranams/index.html.

Kinnane, Derek (1971). Iran bringing literacy and work skills together. *Panorama, 49*: 18-25.

Kluchohn, Clyde (1944). *Mirror for man: A survey of human behavior and social attitudes.* Greenwich, CT: Fawcett Premier Book.

Kohlberg, Lawrence (1971). The concepts of developmental psychology as central guide to education: Examples from cognitive, moral and psychological education. In M.C. Reynolds (Ed.), *Proceedings of the Conference on Psychology and the*

Process of Schooling in the Next Decade (pp. 1-55). Minneapolis: University of Minnesota Press.

LaFramboise, T., Hardin L. K. Coleman & Jennifer Gerton (1995). Psychological impact of biculturalism: Evidence and theory. In Goldberger & Veroff (Eds.), *The culture and psychology reader.* New York: New York University Press.

Lareau, A. (1987). Social class differences in family-school relationships: The importance of cultural capital. *Sociology of Education, 60*: 73-85.

Lautenschlager, Wolfgang (1986). The effects of an overvalued exchange rate on the Iranian economy. *International Journal of Middle East Studies*, 31-52.

Lawrence-Lightfoot, Sara (1999). *Respect.* Massachusetts: Perseus Books.

Lincoln, Y. S. & Guba, E. G. (1985). *Naturalistic inquiry.* Beverly Hills, CA: Sage.

Lipsky, Michael (1980). *Street-level bureaucracy: Dilemmas of the individual in public service.* New York: Russell Sage Foundation.

Loeb, Laurence D. (1977). *Outcaste: Jewish life in southern Iran.* New York: Gordon and Breach.

Longman, Jere (2000, January 16). Soccer: A match with diplomacy on the sideline. The New York Times, Section 8, 4-8.

Lorentz, J. H., & J. Wertime (1980). Iranians. In S. Thernstrom (Ed.), *Harvard encyclopedia of American ethnic groups* (pp. 521-524). Cambridge, MA: Harvard University Press.

Loury, G. (1987). Why should we care about group inequality? *Social Philosophy and Policy, 5*: 249-271.

Mackey, W. F., & Beebe V. N. (1969). *Bilingual schools for a bicultural community: Miami's adaptation to the Cuban refugees.* Rowley, MA: Newbury House.

Mahdi, Ali Akbar (1998). Ethnic idenity among second-generation Iranians in the United States. *Iranian Studies 31*(1), 77-95.

Marshall, C. (1984). Elites, bureaucrats, ostriches, and pussycats: Managing research in policy settings. *Anthropology and Education Quarterly, 15*(3), 235-251.

Marshall, C., & Rossman, G. B. (1989). *Designing qualitative research.* Newbury Park, CA: Sage.

Mashayekhi, A. O. (1992). Acculturation among Iranians in California. Unpublished doctoral dissertation, United States International University.

Matute-Bianchi, M. E. (1986). Ethnic identities and patterns of school success and failure among Mexican-descent and Japanese-American students in a California high school: An ethnographic analysis. *American Journal of Education, 95*: 233-255.

Matute-Bianchi, M. E. (1991). Situational ethnicity and patterns of school performance among immigrant and non-immigrant Mexican-descent students. In M. Gibson & J. U. Ogbu (Eds.), *Minority status and schooling: A comparative study of immigrants and involuntary minorities* (pp. 205-247). New York: Garland.

Maxwell, Joseph A. (1992). Understanding and validity in qualitative research. *Harvard Educational Review 62*(3), 279-300.

Maxwell, J. (1996). *Qualitative research design: An interactive approach.* Thousand Oaks, CA: Sage.

Mead, Margaret (1962). National character. In Sol Tax (Ed.), *Anthropology today: selections* (pp. 396-421). Chicago: University of Chicago Press.

Meleis, Afaf I., Juliene G. Lipson, and Arlene Dallalar (1997). The reluctant immigrant: Immigration experiences among Middle Eastern immigrant groups in Northern California, in *Selected papers on Refugee and Immigrant Issues*, edited by Ruth Krufeld. George Washington University.

Menashri, David (1990). *Iran: A decade of war and revolution.* New York: Holmes and Meier Pulbishers, Inc.

Menashri, David (1992). *Education and the making of modern Iran.* Ithaca: Cornell University Press.

Mendoza, R. H. & J. L. Martinez (1981). The measurement of acculturation. In A. Baron (Ed.), *Explorations in Chicano psychology* (pp. 71-82). New York: Praeger.

Miles, M. B., & Huberman, A. M. (1994). *Qualitative data analysis: An expanded sourcebook.* Thousand Oaks, CA: Sage.

Mitchell, John L. (1999, July 6). Iranians bridging cultural gaps in Beverly Hills; community: immigrants who fled revolution 20 years ago are not moving into mainstream involvement in politics. The Los Angeles Times, part B, page 1.

Mojab, Shahrzad (1991). The state and university: 'The Islamic Cultural Revolution' in the institutions of higher education of Iran,

1980-87. Unpublished doctoral dissertation, University of Illinois at Urbana-Champaign.

Naficy, H. (1991). The poetics and practice of Iranian nostalgia in exile. *Diaspora 1*(3): 285-302.

————. (1993). *The making of exile cultures: Iranian television in Los Angeles.* Minnesota: University of Minnesota Press.

Nyrop, Richard (1978). *Iran: A country study.* Washington, D.C.: The American University.

Ogbu, J. U. & Matutue-Bianchi, M. A. (1986). Understanding sociocultural factors: Knowledge, identity, and social adjustment. *Beyond language: Social and cultural factors in schooling* (pp. 73-142). Sacramento: CA: California State University, Los Angeles, Evaluation, Dissemination and Assessment Center.

Pahlavi, Mohammed Reza (1961). *Mission for my country.* London: Hutchinson.

Parsons, Dana (1988, May 12). Caught in the middle: Iranian immigrants try to blend into American culture without losing identity. *The Los Angeles Times*, part 9, p. 1.

Parsons, Talcott (1966). *Societies: Evolutionary and comparative perspectives.* Englewood Cliffs, NJ: Prentice-Hall.

Pedraza, S. (1996). Cuba's refugees: Manifold migrations. In S. Pedraza & R. G. Rumbaut (Eds.), *Origins and destinies: Immigration, race, and ethnicity in contemporary America* (pp. 263-279). Boston: Wadsworth.

Pedraza, S. and R. G. Rumbaut, Eds. (1996). *Origins and destinies: Immigration, race, and ethnicity in contemporary America.* Boston: Wadsworth.

Pérez, L. (1996). The households of children of immigrants in South Florida: An exploratory study of extended family arrangements. In A. Protes (Ed.), *The new second generation* (pp. 108-118). New York: Russell Sage Foundation.

Pliskin, Karen L. (1987). *Silent boundaries: Cultural constraints on sickness and diagnosis of Iranians in Israel.* New Haven: Yale University Press.

Portes, A., & Stepick A. (1993). *City on the edge: The transformation of Miami.* Berkeley: University of California Press.

Portes, A. (1995). Segmented assimilation among new immigrant youth: A conceptual framework. In R. G. Rumbaut & W. A.

Cornelius (Eds.), *California's immigrant children: Theory,
research, and implications for educational policy* (pp. 71-76). San
Diego: University of California, Center for U.S.-Mexican Studies.

Portes A., & Rumbaut, R.G. (1996). *Immigrant America: A portrait*
(2nd ed.). Los Angeles: University of California Press.

Portes, A. & MacLeod, D. (1996). The educational progress of children
of immigrants: The roles of class, ethnicity, and school context.
Sociology of Education, 69: 255-275.

Portes, A. (Ed.) (1996). *The new second generation.* New York:
Russell Sage Foundation.

Portes, A. and R.G. Rumbaut (in press). *Legacies, the Story of the New
Second Generation.*

Power, Clark F. (1989). *Lawerence Khohlberg's approach to moral
education.* New York: Columbia University Press.

Rachlin, Nahid (1995). *The Heart's Desire: A Novel.* California: City
Light Books.

Rambaud, Marylee Fisher (1996). Respect and child discipline: Low-
income mothers speak. An unpublished dissertation. Harvard
Graduate School of Education.

Rashid, H. M. (1984). Promoting biculturalism in young African-
American children. *Young Children, 39*: 13-23.

Roberts, Steven (1980, November 2). The year of the hostage. *The New
York Times*, Section 6, p. 26.

Rohner, R. P. (1984). Toward a conception of culture for cross-cultural
psychology. *Journal of Cross-Cultural Psychology, 15*, 111-138.

Rosen, M. Barry (Ed.) (1980). *Iran since the revolution.* New York:
Brooklyn College.

Rossman, G. B. (1984). I owe you one. Notes on role and reciprocity in
a study of graduate education. *Anthropology and Education
Quarterly, 15*(3), 225-234.

Royce, A. P. (1982). *Ethnic identity: Strategies of diversity.* Indiana:
University of Indiana Press.

Rucker, Robert E. (1991). Trends in post-revolutionary Iranian
education. *Journal of Contemporary Asia, 21*(4), 455-469.

Rumbaut, Rubén G. (1997). Assimilation and its discontents: Between
rhetoric and reality. *International Migration Review, 31*(4), 923-
960.

Rumberger, R. W. (1983). Dropping out of high school: The influence of race, sex, and family background. *American Educational Research Journal, 20*(2), 199-220.

Sabagh, G., & Bozorgmehr, M. (1987). Are the characteristics of exiles different from immigrants? The case of Iranians in Los Angeles. *Sociology of Social Research, 71*(2), 77-83.

Segall, M. M. (1986). Culture and behavior: Psychology in global perspective. *Annual Review of Pscychology, 37*: 523-564.

Selhoun, Farideh (1983). Iran. Integrateducation, 20 (6): 13-14.

Simpson, John and Tira Shubart (1995). *Lifting the veil: Life in revolutionary Iran.* London: Hodder & Stoughton.

Smith, Terrance (1984, February 12). Iran: Five years of fanaticism. *The New York Times*, p. 21.

Sobhe, Khosrow (1982). Education in revolution: is Iran duplicating the Chinese cultural revolution? *Comparative Education, 18*(3), 271-280.

Sodowsky, G. R. & Carey, J. C. (1988). Relationship between acculturation-related demographics and cultural attitudes of an Asian-Indian immigrant group. *Journal of Multicultural Counseling and Development, 16*: 117-136.

Spence, Micahel A. (1973). Job market signaling. *Quarterly Journal of Economics 87*: 355-374.

Steinberg, L. (1996). *Beyond the classroom.* New York: Simon & Schuster.

Suárez-Orozco, Marcelo, and Carola Suárez-Orozco (1995). *Transformations: Immigration, family life, and achievement motivation among Latino adolescents.* Stanford, CA: Stanford University Press.

Suárez-Orozco, Marcelo (2000). Everything you ever wanted to know about assimilation but were afraid to ask. *Daedalus 129*(4), 1-30.

UNESCO Statistical Yearbook. Paris: UNESCO, 1963, 1974.

Ungar, Sanford (1995). *Fresh blood: The new American immigrants.* New York: Simon & Schuster.

U.S. Bureau of Census (July 1990), The foreign born population in the United States. CP-3-1, Tables 1,3-5, 129-320.

U.S. Commission on Immigration Reform. (1995). Legal immigration: Setting priorities. 1995 Legal immigration report to congress. Washington, D.C.: Author.

U.S. Committee for Refugees (1989). *World refugee survey*. New York: author.

U.S. Department of Justice, Immigration and Naturalization Service (1995). *Statistical yearbook of the Immigration and Naturalization Service*. Washington, D.C.: Author.

Vreeland, Herbert H. (Ed.) (1957). *Iran*. New Haven: Human Relations Area Files.

Wallace, Anthony F. C. (1961). Schools in revolutionary and conservative societies. In Frederick Gruber (Ed.), *Anthropology and Education* (pp. 25-54). Philadelphia, PA: University of Pennsylvania Press.

Warner, Lloyd W., and Leo Srole (1945). *The social systems of American ethnic groups*. New Haven: Yale University Press.

Waters, M. C. (1996). Ethnic and racial identities of second-generation black immigrants in New York City. In A. Portes (Ed.), *The new second generation* (pp.171-196). New York: Russell Sage Foundation.

Wax, R. (1971). *Doing fieldwork: Warnings and advice*. Chicago: University of Chicago Press.

Wescott, Marcia (1990). Feminist criticism of the social sciences. In Joyce McCarl Nielsen (Ed.), *Feminist research methods* (pp. 58-68). Boulder, Colorado: Westview Press.

Westwood, Anthony F. (1965). Politics of distrust in Iran. *The Annals of The American Academy 358*: 123-35.

Wilber, Donald N. (1981). *Iran past and present: From monarchy to Islamic Republic* (9th ed.). NJ: Princeton University Press.

Wright, Robin (1999, July 18). The Iranian Revolution part II comes into focus. *Los Angeles Times*, p. 1.

Zabih, Sepehr (1982). *Iran since the revolution*. Baltimore, Maryland: The John Hopkins University Press.

Zhou, M., & Bankston, C. L., III (1996). Social capital and the adaptation of the second generation: The case of Vietnamese youth in New Orleans. In A. Portes (Ed.), *The new second generation* (pp. 197-220). New York: Russell Sage Foundation.

Zonis, Marvin (1971). *The political elite of Iran*. NJ: Princeton University Press.

Index

urbanization, 26
westoxication, 32, 34
White Revolution, 18
Iranian immigrants, 41-66
    assimilation, 50, 52
    biographies, 64
    diaspora, 41-44, 52
        Australia, 41-43
        Europe, 41, 43, 55
        Israel, 42-43, 55, 66
        Japan, 43
        North America, 43
        Turkey, 41-42, 60
    demographic profile, U.S.,
        41-44
    exiles, 42, 48
    hostage crisis, 8, 11, 33,
        46, 48, 70, 82, 121-
        122
    hostility towards, 8, 10,
        28, 48-50, 126, 163
    intergenerational conflict,
        52
    internal ethnicity, 53
    minorities, 54-60
        Armenians, 57-58
        Bahá'ís, 58-59
        Christians, 59, 159
        Jews, 54-57
        Kurds, 60
        Mashadi Jews, 56-57
        Muslims, 54
        Zoroastrians, 59-60
    national identity, 52, 100
    refugees, 42, 47
    secular Muslims, 47
    social class, 62-64
Methodology, 67-86
    data analysis, 71, 83-85

case ordered
    descriptive meta-
    matrices, 83-85
case study narratives,
    83
    themes, 81-85
data collection, 68, 82,
    167
distrust of researchers, 69,
    72
entry, 69, 72
ethics, 69, 72
epistemological
    framework, 67
informal interviews, 67
interpretive approach, 68,
interview method, 80-82
    location of
    interview,80
    use of Farsi, 81
participants, 81-83
    confidentiality, 75
reflexivity, 69
research design, 67
researcher's role, 67, 69-
    70, 72, 78, 81
    appearance, 71
    cultural broker, 71
sample, 8, 64, 75-77, 79,
    89
    characteristics of, 75
    community center,
    70-71
    educational
    backgrounds, 78-79
    introductions, 74-75
    selection criteria, 77
    occupations of
    parents, 78
site selection, 73